General Sir Michael Rose, commissioned into the Cold selected for the Special Air Service Regiment. Following vice with the SAS in Malaya and Oman, he commanded 22nd SAS Regiment from 1979 to 1982, during which me it was involved in the London Iranian Embassy siege the Falkland Islands War. From January 1994 to uary 1995 he assumed command of the UN Protection ce in Bosnia, after which he became Adjutant General a member of the Army Board. Now retired from Army, he writes and lectures on peace-keeping and ership.

By Michael Rose

Washington's War
Fighting for Peace

Washington's War

From Independence to Iraq

MICHAEL ROSE

PHOENIX

A PHOENIX PAPERBACK

First published in Great Britain in 2007
by Weidenfeld & Nicolson
This paperback edition published in 2008
by Phoenix,
an imprint of Orion Books Ltd,
Orion House, 5 Upper Saint Martin's Lane,
London, WC2H 9EA

An Hachette Livre UK company

1 3 5 7 9 10 8 6 4 2

A CIP catalogue record for this book
is available from the British Library.

ISBN 978-0-7538-2355-2

Typeset at The Spartan Press Ltd,
Lymington, Hants

Printed and bound at Mackays of Chatham plc,
Chatham, Kent

The Orion Publishing Group's policy is to use papers that
are natural, renewable and recyclable products and made
from wood grown in sustainable forests. The logging and
manufacturing processes are expected to conform to the
environmental regulations of the country of origin.

www.orionbooks.co.uk

Contents

Map List

Foreword

by Professor Sir Michael Howard, OM, MC

Once upon a time there was a great nation that, after twenty-five years of conflict, emerged supreme over all its adversaries and prided itself on being the only global superpower. But its tranquillity was disturbed by a group of bloody-minded radicals in a remote corner of the world who resented its hegemony, denied the legitimacy of its rule, and rose in rebellion. The government believed that these trouble-makers could be easily dealt with by firm military action, and set out to do so.

Unfortunately, as Michael Rose points out in this account of the conflict, the government in question 'failed to develop a sufficiently coherent military strategy or even commit sufficient resources to winning the campaign'. Its ministers attempted, from a distance of 3,000 miles, to direct operations in a country, as a contemporary put it, 'of which they have so little knowledge as not to be able to distinguish between good and bad and interested advice'. They sent out too few troops in the first place and denied their generals' repeated requests to send out more. Such forces as they did send easily defeated the rebel forces in the open field, after which their commanders established themselves in comfortable headquarters to maintain the lifestyle to which they were accustomed at home, seldom venturing out to see what was happening in the field. Their troops,

too few to dominate the vast countryside, settled in garrisons where they confined themselves to 'force-protection',
issuing forth occasionally on punitive expeditions whose
brutality lost them such local sympathy as they had hitherto
enjoyed.

The rebels, meanwhile, adopted a strategy of insurgency
that involved avoiding combat against the government's
main forces, but dominating the areas that these were
unable to protect. The inhabitants, whose sympathy for
the rebellion was at first doubtful, found themselves un-
protected by government troops and willy-nilly accepted
the dominance of the insurgents, thereby denying the
government the intelligence it needed for the successful
conduct of its operations.

At home in the metropolis, opposition to the war, at first
silent for fear of appearing unpatriotic and unsupportive of
the armies in the field, gradually became more vocal.
Abroad, the nation's global dominance dwindled to an
unpopular isolation exploited to their advantage by her
former enemies. Eventually the superpower's government
abandoned all attempt to impose its will on the rebellious
region and withdrew its forces. Then both sides lived
happily ever after.

Yes, it is the American War of Independence that
Michael Rose (a.k.a. General Sir Michael Rose, KCB,
CBE, DSO, QGM) describes in this book, and he does so
with all the expertise of a soldier whose experience both of
combat and of high command is virtually unrivalled. But
the analogy with the war that the United States has been
waging in Iraq, with the British as her unhappy allies, is too
close to be ignored, and this similarity is the central theme
of the book.

Like most of his countrymen General Rose is a staunch
supporter and admirer of the United States, but like the rest

of us – and like most Americans – he has been baffled and frustrated by the incompetence with which her political leaders have conducted the war and their inability thereafter to build a viable peace. Point by point he shows how the same hubris and ignorance that led George III to lose the American colonies has guided the American conduct of their war in Iraq, leading to the same dismal results. It is sadly ironic that a nation that won its freedom through a skilful war of insurgency should have proved so helpless when the same strategy was employed against its own armed forces.

General Rose suggests that the best solution would be for the United States to abandon the struggle, as the British did in 1783 and the Americans themselves did in Vietnam, pointing out that both parties revived astoundingly well once they made peace. This may be a shade optimistic. There is little prospect of the United States leaving behind an Iraqi government that is able to create an alternative order once the American troops have left. In the course of fighting for their independence, both the rebellious American colonists and the Viet Cong had created viable states. The Iraqis, at present, seem incapable of doing anything of the sort.

Nevertheless, the president of the United States would do well to recall the reply of the Duke of Wellington when he was asked what was the most difficult task that could face a military commander. 'To know when to retreat,' he replied, 'and to dare to do it.'

Michael Howard, 2007

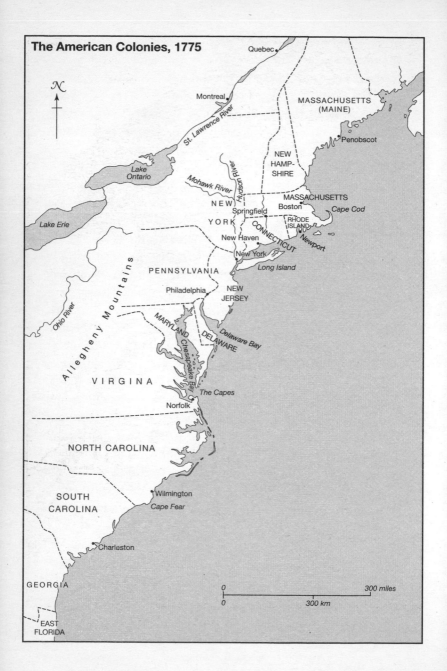

The American Colonies, 1775

Quebec

Montreal

MASSACHUSETTS
(MAINE)

St. Lawrence River

Penobscot

Lake
Ontario

Mohawk River

Hudson River

NEW
HAMP-
SHIRE

Lake Erie

NEW
YORK

Springfield

MASSACHUSETTS

Boston

Cape Cod

RHODE
ISLAND

CONNECTICUT

New Haven

Newport

New York

PENNSYLVANIA

Long Island

Ohio River

Allegheny Mountains

Philadelphia

NEW
JERSEY

MARYLAND

DELAWARE

Delaware Bay

Chesapeake Bay

VIRGINIA

The Capes

Norfolk

NORTH CAROLINA

SOUTH
CAROLINA

Wilmington

Cape Fear

Charleston

GEORGIA

0   300 miles
0   300 km

EAST
FLORIDA

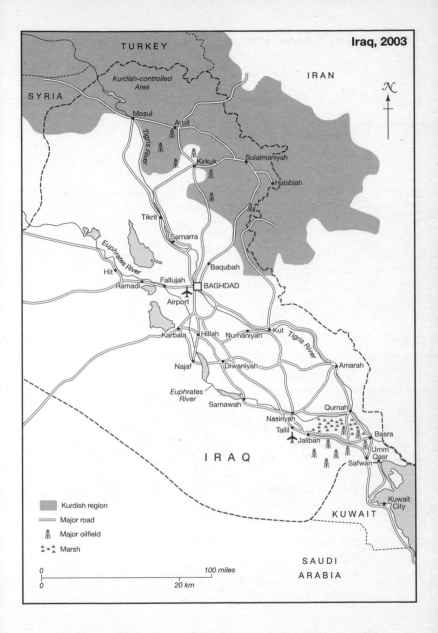

Iraq, 2003

TURKEY

IRAN

SYRIA

Kurdish-controlled Area

Mosul

Arbil

Kirkuk

Sulaimaniyah

Halabjah

Tigris River

Tikrit

Samarra

Euphrates River

Hit

Baqubah

Ramadi

Fallujah

☐ BAGHDAD

Airport

Karbala

Hillah

Numaniyah

Kut

Tigris River

Najaf

Diwaniyah

Amarah

Euphrates River

Samawah

Qurnah

IRAQ

Nasiriyah

Tallil

Jalibah

Basra

Umm Qasr

Safwan

Kuwait City

KUWAIT

Kurdish region

Major road

Major oilfield

Marsh

SAUDI ARABIA

0   100 miles

0   20 km

Washington's War

Preface

A new dynasty gives domination over the ruling dynasty through perseverance, and not through sudden action.

      IBN KHALDUN, fourteenth-century Arab historian

When I first started visiting the battlefields of the American War of Independence, it was well before the 9/11 terrorist attacks had taken place and President Bush had yet to declare global war against Islamic fundamentalist terrorists. My intention had originally been to write an analysis of the military lessons learned by the British Army in what for them had been an unfortunate and ultimately disastrous war. Over the next five years I came to see how great the similarities are between the policies being pursued by America in the present Iraq war and those of Britain in the eighteenth century. Not only do the same political and military imperatives apply, but also George III's inability to recognize what drove the American colonists to rebel against the British Crown is exactly matched by George Bush's lack of understanding of the motivations of Islamic extremist terrorists.

There are of course many obvious differences between the two wars though on closer examination some of these are often not as substantial as they first appear. For example, the level of sectarian violence in Iraq seems much higher today in comparison to the intensity of fighting that took place between the American colonists. In fact, the American War of Independence still remains the second bloodiest conflict in American history in relative terms. The virulence of the propaganda broadcast by the Iraqi insurgents including Al Qaeda also seems to exceed anything put out by the rebels during the American War of Independence. Yet on closer examination, the philosophic justification used by the Boston radicals in their call to arms to the people of the 13 colonies is remarkably similar to that employed by the insurgents in Iraq today. In both wars appeals have been made to the laws of God, interpreted in the one case by the Koran, and in the other by the political theories of John Locke. Indeed, not only did Alexander Hamilton in 1775 refer to the 'sacred rights of man . . . written by the hand of divinity' to justify the rebellion against the British, but the Declaration of Independence is at heart, an extraordinary work of religious and political propaganda.

It would, of course, be absurd to make a comparison between the leadership of George Washington and the founding fathers, with those of the murderous leaders of the Iraqi insurgents. Not only is it hard to discern any central leadership in Iraq today, but George Washington, determined though he was to end British rule in North America, always insisted on adhering to what were the civilised standards of warfare at that time. He condemned atrocities on whichever side they were committed, and admonished anyone who mistreated prisoners. He knew that at some point in the future America would want to extend the noble ideals of liberty and justice throughout the world, and that it would never be able to do this, if the culture from which the new nation was to emerge, had been one of unnecessary bloodshed and savagery.

The notable exception to these similarities is the very different quality of military leadership shown in the two wars. Most senior naval and military commanders on the British side during the American War of Independence proved to be professionally inadequate. That certainly cannot be said for the many American and British officers that I have met in Iraq and elsewhere. They understand far better than I the complexities of modern war and the difficulties that they confront. However those serving in the armies of free democratic nations have to respond to the dictates of their political masters without public comment, no matter how much they may believe the policies and strategies being followed are flawed. They always strive to succeed to the best of their ability, and sadly many of them and their soldiers lose their lives in so doing. It therefore falls on those who have studied history, or who have spent their careers in the military, to point out where politicians decide to ignore the lessons of history and lead their countries into ill-judged wars.

The failure of President Bush and Prime Minister Blair to understand the limitations of military force in combating terrorism undoubtedly stems from their misunderstanding and misrepresentation of the wars in the Balkans that took place between 1992 and 1999. My own experience as the commander of the United Nations Protection Force in Bosnia in 1994 demonstrated to me just how far politicians are prepared to go in their efforts to alter history. Even today, in their speeches, Bush and Blair continually repeat the message that peace was returned to the Balkans by the use of military force, and that efforts at peacekeeping by the United Nations in the region had been ineffective. In this wholly inaccurate analysis, it was the bombing of the Serbs in September 1995 that brought peace at Dayton and it was the bombing of Yugoslavia that removed Milosevic from power in 1999.

Nothing, of course, could be further from the truth. The

decision by the Serbs to sign up to the Dayton peace accord came about, not through NATO bombing, but because the military balance of forces on the ground had been changed by the halting of the fighting between the Muslims and Croats the year before. The two previously warring factions had formed a federation and it was that federation's military success in the autumn of 1995, when they captured much of the territory that the Serbs had wished to trade for peace on their terms, which finally forced the Serbs to bring a halt to the fighting. It had been the UN that had brokered this peace and implemented the peace deal between the two sides.

It had been left to the UN peacekeepers to sustain the people and preserve the state of Bosnia during three and a half years of bloody civil war. Although their mission was limited to the alleviation of human suffering by the delivery of humanitarian aid, the presence on the ground of UN troops was ultimately able to create the conditions in which peace became possible. Without the UN mission, Dayton would never have happened.

But today the propaganda message – that it was force of NATO arms that delivered Dayton, not the UN – is still being plugged by Bush and Blair in their determination to justify the use of military force as the principal means in the war against global terrorists. 'It was NATO that brought serious force to bear and gave the desperately needed muscle to end the war,' claimed Blair in a speech made on the fiftieth anniversary of NATO in 1999. 'In Kosovo we will not repeat those early mistakes made in Bosnia.' Both Bush and Blair clearly remain determined to advance the logic of war.

In spite of their confident assertions, the use of military force in Kosovo also failed to achieve its declared political, humanitarian or military objectives. On 24 March 1999, Javier Solana, then Secretary General of NATO, stated that the objectives of NATO's war against Milosevic were to halt the ethnic cleansing and stop further human suffering in Kosovo. In spite of the most intensive eleven and a half weeks of bombing hitherto experienced in the history of war, 10,000 people were killed and one million people were driven from their homes. When judged on a humanitarian basis, it is clear that the mission failed entirely.

At the same time, General Wesley Clark, the commander of NATO, announced that NATO air power would progressively 'disrupt, degrade, devastate and destroy' the Serb military machine to prevent it from carrying out any further ethnic cleansing. Yet, despite the fact that the Serb Army was equipped with 1950s Soviet technology and that it was exhausted by eight years of war, NATO completely failed to live up to General Clark's expectations. It is estimated that less than twenty Serb armoured vehicles were destroyed in the bombing, and the ethnic cleansing continued at an accelerated pace. When the bombing finally halted, the Serb Army withdrew into Yugoslavia, 'an undefeated army', in the words of the senior British commander on the ground. Bombing simply had not worked. Moreover, NATO failed to deliver any political goals. For it never obtained the freedom of movement throughout Yugoslavia that it had sought at the Rambouillet talks in January 1999. All NATO's other demands had been agreed to by Milosevic.

For British politicians to claim today that the war in Kosovo was a success because NATO 'did, after all, succeed in getting rid of Milosevic', is to indulge in propaganda worthy of Milosevic himself. In reality, Milosevic was kept in power for a further eighteen months as a result of NATO bombing, which collapsed not only the bridges over the River Danube, but also the Serb political opposition. It was the people of Serbia who finally voted Milosevic out of power in the elections of 2001.

In spite of the evident failure of their strategies in the Balkans, the politicians of NATO have reinforced the belief that it is possible to solve complex humanitarian, political and even international security crises through military means. This view has been translated into a doctrine of offensive military action, which has been now been applied in Afghanistan and Iraq. Yet the past clearly shows that military action unsupported by an agreed political frame-work, and one, furthermore, that is backed by adequate economic and social programmes, simply will not endure. Nearly one decade after the end of the Balkan Wars, Euro-pean Union troops are still required to maintain a presence on the ground in order to prevent a return to war. Both Bosnia and Kosovo have become, in effect, protectorates of Europe.

I have discussed the ideas contained in this book exten-sively with military and civilian audiences on both sides of the Atlantic. However, the only people who consistently refuse to discuss the invasion of Iraq and its related stra-tegies have been politicians and their many apologists in the media. The quality of their argument was once well demon-strated to me during a live Channel Four television pro-gramme when I had put forward the view that the recently published September 2002 intelligence dossier, composed as it was of supposition, exaggeration and error, had failed to make a sufficient case for war. I seem to remember that the foreign secretary of the time, Jack Straw, limited his reply to a half-muttered, 'Well, General Rose is entitled to his opinion.'

The same sort of dismissive response from politicians was received by Captain Liddell Hart and General Fuller from politicians after the First World War, when they queried the continuing use of the cavalry and semaphore in battle. They believed that the War Office should think strategically rather than be concerned with tactics, and they suggested that the army should experiment with the combined use of tanks, aircraft and radio communications in order to take advantage of advances in modern technology. Their advice was ignored and they were frequently ridiculed as armchair critics. However, Hitler, Guderian, Manstein and Rommel did choose to listen to Liddell Hart and Fuller, and the technical developments that were introduced into the Wehrmacht nearly brought about the defeat of Britain at the start of the Second World War. The failure of the present US and British administrations to understand the strategic consequences of the changed nature of modern conflict has led to similar deficiencies in effectiveness when it comes to fighting the war against global terrorists.

Unless major changes are made by our politicians to their failing policies in Iraq and Afghanistan, it is certain that the West will face disaster not only in these two countries but also in the wider war against global terrorists. This short book is designed to launch a new debate about when and how we should invite our armed forces to engage in the fight for freedom and democracy in the modern age.

Introduction

> The cause of America is in a great measure the cause
> of all mankind.   THOMAS PAINE, *Common Sense*

The defeat of Lord Cornwallis at the battle of Yorktown in
1781 ended the long, drawn-out effort by the British Crown
to maintain rule over its American colonies. The British
government under Lord North had greatly underestimated
the courage of the American rebels and their determination
to win independence, and also the skill and firmness with
which George Washington was to prosecute the war. The
British had also exaggerated in their minds the willingness
of the American loyalists to fight for the Crown. Above all,
they greatly misunderstood the culture against which they
were fighting, for by 1770 the American colonists were not
looking backwards towards Europe but towards the great
uncharted lands that lay to the west. Although they may
have generally maintained the traditions, religion and legal
practices of the English – and even, on occasion, sent their
children to be educated in England – the majority of the
American settlers felt little obligation or sense of duty
towards their British rulers.

Many of those who began the resistance to British rule
were political activists like Samuel Adams, while others
were Puritans who had grown to distrust all kings and
bishops. Forty years before the Revolutionary War there
had been a spiritual renewal amongst the Protestants on

both sides of the Atlantic called the 'Great Awakening', in which they had rebelled against the established church and its authoritarian structures. They had redefined themselves in moral and spiritual terms and developed an entirely new vision of a future based on individualism and congregational self-government. A generation later their descendants in America were to challenge the existing relationship between the individual and the State, and this culminated in a new wave of colonial radicalism that ultimately could only be satisfied by independence and the founding of a new State based on freedom and democracy. Added to this political movement was the strong economic desire of American colonists to engage in trade freely with the rest of the world and extend their territories to the west across the Ohio River, both of which would require a complete break from British control.

Although they were heavily dependent on trade with Britain, and remained so even after independence, nevertheless the American colonists deeply resented having to pay high rates of British duty, the open racketeering of British customs and excise officials, the corrupt practices of the vice admiralty courts and the increasing use of Royal Navy press-gangs in North American seaports. Many colonists had also speculated heavily in companies that sought to develop the Indian lands to the west of the Allegheny Mountains, in spite of Crown efforts to halt this expansion as a result of agreements that had been made with the Indians during the French and Indian War. Added to this was the arrogance and heavy-handedness of the British, who in the aftermath of their victory against the French in 1763 saw an unrivalled opportunity to impose their will on the rest of the world, including their own colonies.

So passionate was their belief in the ideal of self-determination that the radicals of New England, who today we would call extremists and terrorists, were not only prepared for political confrontation with the British government, but were also ready to risk their property and lives in a war against the most powerful nation in the world. It was the refusal of the British to distinguish between these radical extremists, who demanded full independence, and the more moderate conservative element amongst the American colonists like George Washington that finally drove even the moderates to join forces with the radicals in revolt. As Edmund Burke observed in 1769, 'The Americans have made a discovery, or think they have made one, that we mean to oppress them; we have made a discovery, or think we have made one, that they intend to rise in rebellion . . . we do not know how to advance, they do not know how to retreat.'

The British had simply failed to understand the deep-seated desire for independence that inspired these peoples, especially the New Englanders who were at the heart of the revolutionary agitation. So great was the lack of understanding of what drove the American Revolution that even after the defeat at Yorktown, George III and his politicians were still able to convince themselves that a peace settlement would not necessarily involve a complete break from Britain. A few members of the British Parliament even attributed the rebellious nature of the Americans to the absence of an aristocracy and a class structure, and consequently believed that the rebellion could be extinguished by the simple distribution of honours. Many people in Britain at that time were also convinced that independence and freedom would result in a state of lawlessness and anarchy, since every individual would inevitably seek to take advantage of others. The British could not conceive that an independent, free and civilized society would be able to flourish outside the protection of the Crown, nor did they think that the newly formed Continental Army could provide adequate security for its people against the Indians or invasion from the French or Spanish American colonies.

Yet, as early as 1761, a complete break from Britain was being discussed. John Adams and James Otis, two radical Boston lawyers, were warning that such measures as the Writs of Assistance, which allowed British customs and excise officials to enter at will any private house in the American colonies, violated the rights of man and were therefore void. Adams declared that if necessary he was prepared to 'sacrifice estate, ease, health and applause and even life itself' in order to uphold his rights. In his post-war autobiography he subsequently described the mood of that period with the words: 'England proud of its power and holding Us in Contempt would never give up its pretensions. The Americans devoutly attached to their Liberty, would never submit.' He believed that the flames of American patriotism and the spirit of independence were ignited some fifteen years before the Declaration of Independence was actually signed. Once the revolution had begun in the hearts and minds of the colonial people it would, of course, be hard for them thereafter ever to accept being subjects of an alien crown.

Yet, by the mid eighteenth century, the American colonists generally had a far higher standard of living than most of the people of Britain and Ireland – for it was the latter who had been forced to pay the heavy burden of taxation needed to pay for the defence of North America during the French Indian war. Therefore, in the minds of the American rebels, the War of Independence had always been more about being able to create the political, social and economic conditions in the way that they themselves chose, rather than just being about taxation.

Furthermore, at that time American society was deeply

divided between the rich and poor, the Anglicans and Dissenters, the slaves and slave owners and between the different Native American and immigrant groups that at that time made up the population of the thirteen colonies. The British simply failed to understand and therefore exploit these deep divisions at the political and military level. This critical failure enabled the radicals ultimately to unite, what in fact were widely different groups of people, into supporting the single cause of independence, and probably represents the most serious deficiency of the British counter-insurgency strategy in North America.

In the same way Bush and Blair entirely failed to understand or make use of similarly deep, economic social and tribal differences that divided the peoples in Iraq in 2003. By developing a strategy that identified only three sectarian groups, they effectively split Iraq into three sectarian provinces based on the Sunni, the Shia and the Kurds. After four years of war, their policies brought the country close to civil war in which over three million people have been driven from their homes or have fled abroad as a result of high levels of sectarian violence that the Coalition forces have been quite unable to control.

What had started as a limited insurgency campaign by a small group of radical extremists against the British, who were regarded by 1775 as an alien, foreign occupying power, soon became a fully fledged civil war in which rebel patriots fought Tory loyalists. As in all civil wars, American families were divided, neighbouring communities attacked each other and the terrorist militia groups that roamed the countryside enforcing their political agendas became responsible for some of the worst atrocities committed during the entire war. The attempt by Britain to assert its rule in North America had sparked not only the first popular insurrection to confront the British government outside the British Isles, but also a bloody civil war that was to rage for over eight years. The British had no idea how to respond to the increasing violence that occurred in much of the country, especially in the south. On a wider plane, because the British failed to understand the imperatives that drove the rebellion and continued to believe that the few rebels and miscreants who were causing trouble in the colonies could be quickly and easily dealt with by firm military action, they did not develop a sufficiently coherent military strategy or ever commit enough resources to winning the campaign.

The similarities to America's approach to the insurgency in Iraq and also to the wider war against global terrorists are striking. Both were wars of choice and both wars sprang from competing ideologies. In the same way that George III thought civilized society was only possible under royal protection, today President Bush and Prime Minister Blair believe that civilized society can only properly flourish where conditions of democracy and freedom exist. In this Messianic view, no other values are capable of fulfilling human potential. As a result America, supported by Britain, feels that it has a duty, in the words of George Bush, to use its exceptional military might to 'seek a balance of power that favors human freedom: conditions in which all nations and all societies can choose for themselves the rewards and challenges of political and economic liberty'. Bush and Blair believe that these values are right and true for every person and every society on this planet. It is inconceivable to them that there may exist people and societies who have entirely different values and ideals, who may have other notions of what constitutes freedom and good governance, or who may choose to develop these ideals in their own way and at another time.

It is already quite clear that Bush and Blair's singular Western view of what constitutes the necessary conditions for civilized society is not accepted by everyone, particularly by those Muslims who will always place a greater value on religious belief than on Western concepts of individual freedom or forms of political structure. They do not believe that Western liberal-style democracy is necessary to their personal fulfilment or to good governance – since these can best be obtained through adherence to their religion, family and tribe, and obedience to their hereditary ruler. For Muslims, God's law, as revealed in the Koran, dictates every act of daily living as well as worship. It does not make any distinction between religion and the secular. Their concepts of freedom, justice and human dignity derive from the rules of Islam – not from Western ideology. It makes no sense therefore for the West to attempt to impose its secular ideals on such a society. Furthermore, for societies based on tribal structures, as many Arab countries are, 'one man one vote' represents a clear threat to the interests of the minority tribes. In these societies, everyone has the traditional right to appeal directly to their hereditary ruler for justice. All this means that the determination of America and Britain to enforce their fundamental view on the world through military action inevitably brings them into armed confrontation with those who follow the path of Islam, for Islam also demands that Muslims defend their faith when it is threatened.

When the American colonists were faced with extinction by the French and Indians in the middle of the eighteenth century, they were grateful for British military protection. However, when that threat disappeared in 1763 with the signing of the Peace of Paris, the colonists no longer wanted British troops garrisoning their towns or, indeed, stationed in their country. What had originally been a welcome army of protection quickly became an occupying force whose purpose in many American minds was to coerce the

colonists into accepting a continuance of British parliamentary rule. In the same way, the people of present-day
Iraq, who were so grateful to the Coalition forces for the
removal of Saddam Hussein, rapidly turned against the
foreign occupiers once their tyrannical ruler had been
toppled from power. Their initial gratitude had never
implied an acceptance of Western political ideals. Nor did
it mean that Iraqis would accept the long-term presence in
their country of the Coalition forces, whom they perceive as
infidels – for Iraq contains some of the most holy Islamic
sites after Mecca and Medina. It is significant that when
general elections were held in Iraq in 2005, they were
contested by 141 political parties, and the Iraqi people
voted almost wholly in accordance with their tribal and
religious loyalties, not for any particular political ideology.
The elections therefore had the effect of entrenching sectarian positions and dividing rather than uniting Iraq.
Specifically, the introduction of the concept of democracy
into Iraq and the de-Ba'athification process directly threatened the supremacy and identity of the western Iraq Sunni
tribes, a people who have controlled Iraq for centuries. And,
of course, it was the Sunnis who most fiercely resisted the
occupation, just as the people of Massachusetts had done
against the British two and a quarter centuries before, when
their identity had been so threatened.

The war in North America was a people's war in that
large numbers of the colonists participated in rebellion
against the colonial power, but it was never a truly revolutionary war in the Marxist sense. The withdrawal of the
British did not bring about a complete overthrow of the
existing economic or social structures within the thirteen
colonies, which remained elitist and aristocratic and continued to be dominated by American landowners, lawyers
and merchants. Nor, at a political level, did the revolution

result in the people rising up and seizing power, as happened during the French Revolution. For although the membership of the state legislatures became far more representative of the common people after independence, there still was no universal suffrage. Indeed, slavery continued in America until after the Civil War and it is arguable that full civil rights for all Americans were only achieved in 1954.

The secret Constitutional Convention held in Philadelphia in 1787 to work out the relationship between the states and the federal government resulted in a tightening rather than a loosening of central political control. Although the delegates to the Convention were chosen by the state legislatures, it nevertheless gave the new federal government powers to levy taxes, borrow money and establish uniform duties and excise taxes. These powers were, of course, not far removed from those that had been wielded by the British Parliament and they challenged the notion of government of the people through the states for which many radicals such as Patrick Henry had fought. The Convention had been a victory of the conservative elite over popular government.

Furthermore, in spite of the 12 million acres that were taken from the Tories after the war and handed out to small farmers in New York, traditional landowners elsewhere were able to greatly extend their already sizeable landholdings, as long as they had not fought against the revolution. Few did this more successfully than George Washington. Even English families who had remained neutral during the war, such as the Clarkes of Hyde Hall in New York, did not always have their lands sequestered by the state. It was therefore economic self-interest that had driven the rebellion in North America as much as religious fervour or the pursuit of democracy and freedom. Indeed, the revolutionary ideals of liberty and equality would have to wait for the French Revolution in 1789 before they took root in Europe. And it was to be another seventy years before all men were to be truly born free in America.

Across the Atlantic, the defeat of the British by the insurgents in North America probably produced a greater political and social transformation. It ended Britain's position as the unchallenged global superpower and brought about parliamentary changes that were to culminate in the great Reform Act of 1832. This Act enfranchised the middle classes and halted the corruptions, sinecures and patronages of the British political and administrative system. It also brought about a fundamental change in the way the British Army went to war with regard to doctrine and tactics. For although the consequences of victory may be glory and honour, with defeat there comes recrimination and a revolution in military affairs. It is no accident that only twenty-five years after its withdrawal from North America, the British Army was able to successfully wage war against Napoleon in the Peninsular War, using the insurgency tactics it had learned in North America.

In the middle of the eighteenth century, the British Army was considered to be one of the best fighting forces in the world. Its doctrine and tactics had been forged at Dettingen and Minden and it had become unequalled in Europe for the steadfastness of its infantry in battle and its use of artillery. In relative terms, it was like the modern American Army in its unrivalled status. But it was an army that had been manned, trained and equipped to fight a general war in Europe and it was therefore entirely unsuited to fight an insurgency campaign, especially one that had to be waged at long distance in the uncharted forests of North America. The current US Army has, of course, been trained primarily to fight a conventional war rather than an insurgency, and this has undoubtedly created problems for its soldiers in Iraq.

It is not surprising that the British generals in North America – men such as Howe, Burgoyne, Clinton and Cornwallis – should have felt supremely confident of their ability to defeat what they considered to be an insignificant group of rebels. 'I may safely assert', wrote Howe in 1775, 'that the insurgents are very few, in comparison with the whole of the people.' In a letter written as late as August 1778 Lord George Germain, the Secretary for America, was still describing the rebels as being 'but a contemptible body of vagrants, deserters and thieves'.

The British, therefore, not only failed to understand the strategy and tactics needed to win an insurgency war, but also greatly underestimated the resilience and determination of the relatively small number of American revolutionaries, who at the start of the war were supported at most by a third of the colonial population. Over time, of course, like other insurgent groups, they would be able to persuade the majority to support their cause, often by brutal intimidation. It was this small group of American insurgents that was to teach the British Army lessons about insurgency warfare that are still enshrined in British military doctrine in the twenty-first century.

In contrast, in Iraq Bush seemed to be following the same political and military route as was taken by the British in the eighteenth century. For the American administration has also greatly underestimated the determination of the Iraqi people to rid themselves of a foreign army of occupation. In 2003, Secretary of Defense Donald Rumsfeld dismissed the Iraqi insurgents as being no more than a few terrorists and Islamic extremists, referring to them more than a year after the invasion of Iraq as 'dead-enders . . . those remnants of the defeated regime'. A year later, on 19 March 2004,

President Bush continued the dismissive rhetoric by stating, 'There are still violent thugs and murderers in Iraq, and we're dealing with them.' Yet, by the spring of 2007, nearly 3,000 American soldiers and possibly half a million Iraqi civilians had been killed. Progress towards creating a democratic and economically viable state in Iraq remained stalled, and as the country drifted towards civil war, American words were beginning to sound like a ghastly echo of Germain.

At the strategic level the Bush administration still seemed to believe that US military power would always prevail, no matter what sort of war is being fought. For current US military doctrine advocates the application of offensive power to win all wars, and even when engaged in nation-building operations, the US Army is expected to follow a warfighting doctrine that demands it must first gain the initiative, build momentum and finally win decisively through the application of combat power. As the British found in the eighteenth century, America discovered in Vietnam and the Russians realized in Afghanistan, this is simply not possible when fighting insurgency wars.

In their field manuals US Army commanders are warned that the use of force must always be consistent with policy objectives and that the use of excessive force in stabilization operations may lead to a loss of sympathy and support amongst the local populace. But an analysis of US-led operations on the ground in Iraq during the first four years of the war suggests that these constraints have not been universally followed. For example, the killing and injuring of 200 unarmed civilians by soldiers of the 82nd Airborne Division shortly after it arrived in Fallujah on 28 April 2003 undoubtedly caused many Iraqis to take sides against the Coalition forces. Whatever the tactical benefits of the subsequent US Marine assaults on Fallujah that took place in 2004, they were extremely damaging to American interests at the strategic level. This is because the inevitable scenes of suffering and destruction caused by the battles in Fallujah resulted in the widespread alienation of Muslims around the world. Until these events, Muslims had been prepared to see how the Americans behaved in what was after all a brother Muslim country. After 2004, it was inevitable that many saw the American-led occupation force as oppressive and brutal.

During the insurgency in North America, the same negative consequences resulted from the harsh punitive measures taken by British troops against civilian communities. Incidents like the burning of churches at New Haven and Fairfield by General Tryon in 1779 or the massacre by the British of 113 surrendered American rebels at Waxhaw in Virginia on 29 May 1780 persuaded large numbers of hitherto uncommitted Americans to side with the insurgents. This undoubtedly turned the tide against the British, especially in the south, and thereby cost them the entire war. The widespread support for the rebellion also proved to be an important factor in deciding foreign powers such as France, Spain and Holland that they should support the American revolutionaries against the British.

In general war, the principal object of an army is decisively to defeat its opponent using overwhelming force. Destruction of the enemy's command structure and fighting capability is vital to the successful outcome of the mission. Seizing the initiative using surprise, aggression and speed is centrally important to success in modern conflict. The civilian population is something to be avoided, not engaged, by fighting armies. But the doctrine of general war has little relevance to counter-insurgency warfare situations. For in such wars, winning the support of the population is always the key objective, not seizing ground or destroying an army. Since the insurgents generally retain the initiative, a key objective of any counter-insurgency strategy is to obtain intelligence about the organization, capabilities and intentions of the insurgents. This can only be done when the mass of the population is mobilized in support of the established government and are prepared to provide it with the necessary intelligence. If the government of the day loses popular support, it will lose the war. A government and army engaged in a counter-insurgency campaign must therefore derive their inspiration and doctrinal thinking more from the writings of Che Guevara than from those of Clausewitz. It must develop a long-term strategy aimed at winning the support of the populace, which includes all the political, economic, social and sometimes religious elements of government administration. At the tactical level, the use of overwhelming military force is inevitably counterproductive in counter-insurgency campaigns.

Changing attitudes and winning the information battle always remain more important than changing regimes. Since the ability to provide security to the civilian population is central to any counter-insurgency mission, large numbers of troops are needed to provide a permanent presence on the ground in order to protect them. The people simply will not side with a government if their families and livelihood are being continually threatened by insurgents. Thus, the provision of adequate security remains a vital component of any counter-insurgency strategy. As George Washington explained during the American War of Independence, people 'will expect the Continental Army to give what support they can – or failing this, they will cease to depend upon or support a force from which no protection is given'.

During the American War of Independence, the British were never able to properly support the loyalists or even protect the uncommitted American colonists from intimidation by the colonial insurgents. Similarly, following the invasion of Iraq in 2003, the Coalition forces have never been able to provide sufficient protection either to the general population or, importantly, to the Iraqi security forces, many of whom as a result have now sided with the insurgents. It was the US Secretary of Defense Donald Rumsfeld who made the disastrous but quite deliberate decision to commit only limited numbers of troops to Operation Iraqi Freedom. In doing so, he totally failed to understand or take account of the true nature of the conflict to which he had committed his nation. The consequence of this extraordinary decision was that the Coalition forces were never able to establish sufficient control of the Iraqi population during the immediate and chaotic post-war phase in Iraq – and it was specifically this shortcoming that allowed the insurgency to develop so rapidly. Four years after the fall of Saddam Hussein, as insurgent militias fight each other for control, Iraq is clearly hovering on the edge of civil war.

One can compare America's decision to disband the Iraqi police and army with the British failure to organize the loyalist militias in North America, for both occurrences led to a critical shortage of troops. In the eighteenth century, Britain simply did not have sufficient military resources to fight an insurgency war in North America and at the same time defend its Empire. As a result the British could not succeed in the two priority tasks that always confront an occupying power in any counter-insurgency campaign: safeguarding the population and defeating the insurgents. Therefore, throughout the entire Revolutionary War, Britain would always remain dependent on American loyalist support for victory, but because of its flawed policies, this support would never be forthcoming in sufficient quantities. At a strategic level, the British had committed themselves to an unwinnable war – just as the Americans were to do two and a quarter centuries later. The War of Independence, using General Zinni's description of the Iraq war, was 'the wrong war, fought in the wrong place, at the wrong time'.

During the past twenty-five years, a fundamental change has occurred in the nature of conflict that has led America to look away from counter-insurgency wars. The technological military advances that were developed to defeat the Soviet Union enable the US armed forces to rapidly identify and destroy any conventional force that opposes them. The average time between identifying a target and destroying it is today measured in minutes rather than days – something that is unique in the history of war. This great American technical superiority has been clearly demonstrated in both Afghanistan and Iraq, where the destruction of the Taliban's and Saddam Hussein's conventional military forces was as quick as it was complete. The consequence of these remarkable victories is far-reaching. No potential adversary is ever likely to present itself conventionally to American firepower: if it did so it would be destroyed. Wars in the twenty-first century, therefore, are more likely to take the form of insurgencies than general wars. In this form of war the enemy remains concealed amongst the civilian population and only operates against a conventional army when local superiority can be gained. Simple weapons are employed and great reliance is placed on the element of surprise.

Today's adversary strikes at political, economic, cultural and civilian targets. The attacks by al-Qaeda against economic and government targets in America on 11 September 2001, the use of suicide bombers by Palestinian terrorists against civilian and military targets, and the rocket attacks into Israel mounted by Hezbollah in 2006 provide good examples of this new form of conflict. Insurgents know that they cannot win by military means. They will therefore seek to undermine the political will of their opponents through protracted conflict, which will be asymmetric in nature. The Iraqi insurgents well understand the principles of insurgency warfare. They know that they cannot take on the Coalition forces in set-piece battles and so have adopted the tactics of the guerrilla fighter. In so doing, the Iraqi insurgents were quickly able to gain the military initiative through the use of snipers, suicide bombers and simple roadside explosive devices that are able to destroy sophisticated armoured vehicles. For every electronic countermeasure, the Iraqis, with the help of Iran, have been able to develop effective electronic counter-countermeasures.

This is exactly what the American insurgents did during the Revolutionary War in the eighteenth century. After the battle of Germantown in 1777, George Washington was compelled to accept that the Continental Army could not engage in formal combat with the British Army – and so he decided to fight a war of insurgency. He saw that the civilian population of America constituted the vital ground in the war – not the territory of the thirteen colonies – even if this approach meant giving up the capital city of the United States, Philadelphia. He was to obtain his technical expertise in gunnery and combat engineering from the French, just as the Iraqi insurgents today obtain their technical expertise from sympathizers abroad.

It is clear that because of their great reliance on military technology, the US armed forces are finding it extremely difficult to fight a campaign in which success does not depend on superiority of firepower. As General Nash, commander of the US Army 1st Armoured Division, put it after a six-month tour of operations in Bosnia, 'I have trained thirty years to read a battle field . . . now you are asking me to read a peace field. It doesn't come easy. It ain't natural. It ain't intuitive. They don't teach this stuff at Leavenworth.' Even after four years of unsuccessful war, many Americans clearly still believed that it was possible to deliver the original objectives of the mission in Iraq by using ever higher levels of military force in response to the mounting difficulties that they face. As a result, the high number of civilian casualties inflicted by the Americans in the first four years of the occupation, combined with the revelations about Abu Ghraib prison and the existence of Camp Delta at Guantanamo Bay, has greatly strengthened the resistance to the continuing presence of the American force.

The American and British political leaders remained continually in denial about the true situation in Iraq, just as their predecessors George III and Lord Germain continued to deny the failing nature of their war strategy in North America. Only six months before the final capitulation at the Battle of Yorktown, Germain wrote to George III confidently stating, 'So very contemptible is the rebel force now in all parts, and so great is our superiority everywhere, that no resistance on their part is to be apprehended that can materially obstruct the process of the King's arms in the speedy suppression of the rebellion.' In their speeches, Bush and Blair for too long emphasized small items of progress and ignored the wider deteriorating situation. In April 2005, two years after the invasion at a time when the country was evidently sliding towards civil war, Dick Cheney was still claiming, 'We're making major progress. Iraq is in the last throes of, if you will, the insurgency.' In a speech to the prime minister of Iraq in July 2006, President Bush cited the handover of a province to the Iraqi forces as an example of progress. In fact the province in question, Muthanna, had only ever been garrisoned by 250 British troops and their presence there had been symbolic.

Whenever opposition parties on either side of the Atlantic have questioned the conduct of the war in Iraq they have invariably been silenced by the argument that to speak out against the war amounts to treason, being unpatriotic or not supporting the soldiers in the front line. This same argument, of course, was successfully used by the Tories against the Whigs in British parliamentary debates during the American War of Independence. It was only when Britain was faced by final defeat that the Whigs were able to sweep aside objections and a more hard-nosed logic prevailed.

The political and economic costs of the war in Iraq are likely to become as difficult for the US government to sustain as they were for the government of Lord North. Ultimately, it will be the wider strategic consequences of the war for America that will bring to an end hostilities in Iraq – just as they ended the American War of Independence for the British. As early as 1781, after six years of indecisive conflict and the loss of Cornwallis's army at Yorktown, the British government had decided that 'we cannot raise another army', and sued for peace. Although theoretically they would have been able to continue the war against the American rebels, since they still had 30,000 troops deployed in America, their long-term strategic and imperial interests elsewhere in the world were being too greatly damaged in what was not a vital area of British interest. Lord Shelburne, who was by then prime minister, therefore persuaded George III to abandon the British effort to maintain his rule in the thirteen North American colonies. The Treaty of Paris, giving full independence to America, was finally signed in 1783.

The current US-led occupation of Iraq, and the adverse

propaganda that it generates, is doing grave damage to the chances of winning the wider war against global terrorism. It is therefore likely that the Americans will have to withdraw sooner, rather than later, from Iraq if their country is to preserve its global position as a superpower. For in the same way that France, Spain and Holland were able to mount a challenge to Britain while it was focused on the insurgency in North America, so China and India are today taking full advantage of President Bush's obsession with the war in Iraq.

George Washington, who was commander-in-chief of the Continental Army throughout the Revolutionary War – and who was to become the first president of the United States – was, like George Bush, a man of strong conviction. Indeed, both share a passionate belief in the goodness of freedom. But unlike his forty-second successor, George Washington was able to combine his idealism with practical military experience – for when Virginia had been threatened by the French during the Seven Years War, Washington had volunteered for military duty. As a result, he had been able to see at first hand how the Indians employed guerrilla tactics against the British regular troops. He had begun to understand the essentials of insurgency warfare. If George Bush had felt the same sense of duty as his predecessor and had himself experienced military service in Vietnam, then he too might have better appreciated the sort of war to which he was committing his nation in Iraq – and, more widely, how to more effectively prosecute the war against global terrorism.

It was George Washington's military skill and firm conviction in the justice of his cause that were to sustain him through many years of adversity visited upon him by the British and also his own Congress, with whom he had had to argue incessantly in order to obtain sufficient resources to fight the war. His objection to British rule was based on Christian principles of natural justice and freedom – concepts that had already been firmly implanted in the American colonies by the English. Initially, he had not thought that independence was the certain outcome of the dispute over taxation between America and the British Parliament. As he wrote to an English friend in 1774, Captain Mackenzie, who believed that the people of Massachusetts were preparing for a rebellion against the Crown, 'Independence is neither the wish nor the interest of that colony, nor of any other on the continent, separately or collectively; but at the same time you may make certain that none of them will ever submit to the loss of those privileges, of those precious rights, which are essential to the happiness of every free state, and without which liberty, property, life are deprived of every security.'

It is clear that Washington was no radical revolutionary in the image of Robespierre or Danton, having been brought up as a member of the American landowning classes. Even after hostilities had commenced in 1775 when rebels fired on British troops at Lexington and Concord, he still did not think that a split from Britain was inevitable. The thirteen colonies remained divided on this issue, for while in New England there was strong support for the rebellion, in Maryland and Georgia in the south the revolutionaries were in a minority, and New York actually sent significant reinforcements to the help of the British. It was the genius of George Washington, like Oliver Cromwell before him, that in the end he came to believe that freedom from the Crown was essential if America was to develop its full potential. 'Unhappy it is', he wrote, 'to reflect that as brother's sword has been sheathed in a brother's breast and that the once happy and peaceful plains of America are either to be drenched in blood or inhabited by slaves.

Sad alternative, but can a virtuous man hesitate in his choice?'

In wars, when families and former friends are set against each other all morality breaks down, and hatred and a desire for vengeance can become an overwhelming motivation for further killing. Yet George Washington never lost his sense of humanity and always understood that when the war ended, people would have to live side by side with one another. On another occasion he wrote, 'I think or at least I hope that there still exists amongst us sufficient public virtue.' As the great American republic that the original thirteen colonies subsequently became demonstrates today, George Washington's hopes were to be amply justified. It was their enlightened political views that distinguishes the North American radicals and insurgents during the eighteenth century from the brutal and somewhat cosmic ideological aspirations of Al Qaeda extremists today.

The political differences between Britain and the American rebels were not exclusively about taxation without representation. The desire for independence from the Crown was also driven in part by the economic need to develop lands to the west. At the end of the Seven Years War, during which time the Iroquois Indians had fought mostly for the British against the French, George III had agreed with the Indians to limit the extent of the western boundaries of the American colonies. He had done this to reward their loyalty and so the Proclamation Line of 1763 had forbidden settlements west of the Allegheny Mountains. However, many colonists like George Washington were determined to ignore this edict. Prices of tobacco were falling in America and, like many other established Virginian planter families, he desperately needed alternative sources of income. In 1763 – the very year of the Proclamation – he had set up the Mississippi Land Company, with the express aim of developing settlements along the Ohio River. He regarded the Proclamation as 'a temporary expedient to quieten the minds of the Indians', and suggested to his agent and surveyor William Crawford that he survey the prospective settlements 'under the pretence of hunting other game'. Five years later, his assessment that the British Crown could not hold this position proved correct when the Crown agreed a new treaty with the Iroquois that drew the boundary line further west. This allowed George Washington to redeem the promise of land that had been made to all colonial soldiers who had served in the Seven Years War, and he ended up with 24,000 acres of valuable land along the Ohio River.

It is ironic, therefore, that the greatest imperial power in the world, Great Britain, should have fought a war in America that tried to stem the imperialistic tendencies of the colonial settlers. Nevertheless, and with the benefit of hindsight, it is indeed fortunate for the subsequent history of the world that the British were compelled to give the Americans their independence – for it is exceedingly unlikely that the pioneering spirit and sense of enterprise that characterizes America today would have developed so swiftly or well under the yoke of the British Crown. Independence not only permitted America to continue to expand to the west, at a rate of some 17 miles a day, but also allowed it to become the benevolent superpower that it is today – and one that came to Britain's rescue twice in the last century.

If present-day Britain is not the great power that it once was, it has undoubtedly maintained many of the qualities that made it once great – not least in the British military ability to fight counter-revolutionary wars. As Britain fights alongside the Americans in Iraq, it is clear that the considerable differences in doctrine that are evident between the two nations began to emerge immediately after the end of the American War of Independence. America became determined never to be beaten militarily again by a superior army, and so started the process of building a military capability in warfighting that is unequalled in the world today. Being on the winning side in two World Wars confirmed the American military strategists' view that developing conventional combat power was the correct policy to follow. If American confidence was dented by the Vietnam War experience, this was quickly repaired in the lightning successes of the Cold War, the first Iraq war and in Afghanistan. However, the emphasis on conventional warfighting doctrine did not make the US good at fighting counter-insurgency-level campaigns.

Britain, on the other hand, continued to develop the doctrine and skills for fighting small wars – even though after the American War of Independence the British had to engage almost immediately in global conflict during the Napoleonic Wars. The subsequent experience of small wars gained by Britain in maintaining its colonies – particularly in India and Africa – kept these skills live. Today, the British Army's success in defeating the IRA in Northern Ireland and the contribution that it has made to UN peacekeeping operations in the Balkans largely derive from the lessons that it learned between 1775 and 1783. In the absence of a large-scale warfighting capability, the British Army has tried to understand the fundamental elements that drive insurgency wars, and develop strategies and tactics that are able to deal with them.

This book, therefore, is about the legacy of George Washington, the different approaches of America and Great Britain towards countering insurgency warfare and how these are being played out in Iraq today.

Chapter One

The New England colonies are in a state of rebellion . . . blows must decide.   GEORGE III, 1774

Containment is not possible . . . we must take the battle to the enemy.

PRESIDENT GEORGE BUSH, 2002

In the eighteenth century, wars tended to be lengthy, somewhat indecisive affairs. Armies spent much of their time marching and countermarching about the countryside without much effect. The object of a campaign was not necessarily, in the words of Sir John Fortescue, 'to seek out an enemy and beat him', but to force the opponent to run out of money and supplies. The deciding factors in war were generally financial and logistical, rather than rare but bloody encounters on the battlefield in which the use of overwhelming military force decided the day. In his sequence of battles from Blenheim to Malplaquet when Marlborough sought to bring the French Army to battle and destroy it, he had been the exception rather than the rule in eighteenth-century warfare. When armies did meet, infantry tactics consisted of massed ranks halting at 50 yards range and discharging musket volleys at an opposing force – often with little effect. The musket was an inaccurate weapon and slow to fire and reload. To maintain a high rate of fire, it was thus necessary to develop precise drills in which one rank fired while the other ranks reloaded. Only *in extremis* did a bayonet charge take place either to destroy the enemy or drive him from the battlefield. Artillery and cavalry were mainly used in support of the infantry during battle to cause attrition to the enemy. They were rarely deployed on their own.

Occasionally, armies employed light irregular forces as scouts and flank guards to protect the movements of the heavier infantry. They were not regarded as individual combat arms and rarely manoeuvred on their own. These irregular forces tended to be raised in time of war and were disbanded immediately after the war had ended. The Austrians had recruited such forces amongst the Croats and Serbs in the seventeenth century during their wars against the Ottoman Empire in the Balkans, and Marshal de Saxe of France had also made extensive use of light infantry during the twelve-year War of Spanish Succession that ended in 1713. But the permanent establishment of light infantry as separate manoeuvre units did not spread to other European armies until the Seven Years War.

By the mid eighteenth century, the British Army had been closely modelled on the Prussian Army by the Duke of Cumberland, who was a disciple of Frederick the Great. The Peace of Paris, which ended the Seven Years War in 1763, had left Britain unchallenged by any other power. The British had soundly defeated their enemies, and their main ally, Prussia, was a small, sparsely populated country that had exhausted itself supporting the vast military ambitions of Frederick the Great. The British Army may have been regarded as the best in the world but its generals had failed to learn the lessons of the Prussian defeat at Kolin in 1757, when a light force of Austrians had defeated a greatly superior army by the use of flanking fire. As a result of this disaster, Frederick decided to copy the tactics of the

Austrians and raised a force of Jägers, which was not only able to deliver accurate rifle fire, but was also highly manoeuvrable. He had come to see that light infantry could be an alternative to the formations of heavy infantry when it came to winning battles. The British Army did not follow his example. Although some experiments in the use of light infantry were carried out on Salisbury Plain in 1774 under William Howe, who was later to become the commander-in-chief in North America, light infantry in the American War of Independence was used only as flanking companies rather than as a separate combat arm.

Between the end of the Seven Years War in 1763 and the start of the American War of Independence, the strength of the British Army had inevitably been much reduced – with the British government taking the traditional view that British interests could best be secured by maintaining a large naval fleet capable of defeating the French. This strategy also depended on being able to dissuade the Spanish and Dutch from siding with the French in any future war with the British. At that time, the British Army numbered no more than 45,000 strong – made up of twenty-seven cavalry and seventy-seven infantry regiments. The role of the British Army during this period was in theory no different from what it traditionally had been: general war, policing and training. However, it was seriously overstretched by the need to garrison a growing Empire, which now included North America, the West Indies, India, Gibraltar and Minorca. Regiments were therefore frequently stationed abroad for long periods, during which time they became much reduced through illness or desertion – for training in these remote stations was virtually non-existent. The British Army was also required to maintain a large standing force in Ireland. However, this force had fallen into such poor condition that it was, as Sir

Ralph Abercromby, its commander-in-chief, once famously remarked, 'in a state of licentiousness which must render it formidable to everyone but the enemy'.

In 1756, a major expansion of the army had taken place, with fifteen battalions being sent to North America to defend the colonies from the French, who were claiming territories to the west of the Ohio River. However, this rapid expansion produced an army with a high number of recruits whose only training was on the actual field of battle. This was to happen again during the subsequent American War of Independence.

The British Army was generally quite ill-prepared for the difficult conditions or type of enemy that were to confront it in North America. For most of the eighteenth century the army had suffered greatly from a severe shortage of money and, importantly, it had lacked sufficient time to train for general war. When not campaigning in the Low Countries, it spent much of its time on internal security duties – marching from town to town in Britain maintaining order – or in garrison duties abroad. Much of what little training the soldiers received consisted of perfecting drills on the parade ground – for example, forming ranks from the line of march. Such drills were very intricate and consequently slow and unwieldy. On one occasion the Duke of Cumberland stated how proud he had been to witness a regiment forming ranks in only ten minutes. Insufficient ammunition and ball was issued for live firing, so once again much time was spent on practising complicated firing drills on the square. Of the battalions that arrived in North America during the Seven Years War, only a handful had previously trained together as a formed unit.

The dreadful defeat of a British expeditionary force commanded by the ill-starred General Braddock in July 1755 by a handful of Indians supported by French troops at

Monongahela (near modern-day Pittsburgh, Pennsylvania) did nothing to alter British tactics or prepare them for the counter-insurgency war that was to be fought in North America twenty years later. However, one of the few survivors of this expeditionary force was a young Virginian captain called George Washington. He had observed just how difficult it was to form ranks from the line of march – especially when the attacking enemy were Indian skirmishers hidden in the forest on either side of the road. From these positions the Indians had been able to pour deadly fire into the flanks of the British without any effective response by the redcoats, who were forced to fire blindly into the surrounding bushes at an unseen enemy. Many of the casualties amongst the British troops were caused by this wild firing.

Washington also saw how slow and unwieldy a British force trained and equipped for European warfare could be, with its cumbersome artillery and endless lines of pack horses, wagon trains and powder carts. It had even been necessary for Braddock to take with him carpenters and sailors from British Navy ships to help construct a road through the virgin forest along which this force could progress – often at speeds of no more than 5 miles per day. It was clearly not possible to manoeuvre such a large force with any speed, and the key element in battle – that of surprise – would generally be absent. Having seen the shortcomings of the British Army during the Seven Years War, Washington was able to build a Continental Army that could cover great distances in short periods of time. This capability was probably best demonstrated by Washington's long march from New York to Yorktown in September 1781.

Possibly the most conspicuous critic of the traditional British strategy of attritional warfare in the eighteenth century, however, was Major Robert Rogers, a native of New Hampshire, who in 1756 had recruited nine companies of American colonists to fight for the British during the French and Indian War. He had adapted the characteristics of the frontier war against the Indians and developed them into a new approach to warfare in which lightly armed irregular troops could be effectively used against regular formations of the enemy. Accompanied by his Rangers, he was to play a key role in the British campaign to drive the French from Canada during the next four years – reconnoitring French positions, attacking supply convoys and leading raids deep into enemy territory. On one occasion he led an expeditionary force of 200 men into Canada, during which time he covered over 400 miles in two months. At the end of the war his force, along with others, was disbanded, as British commanders considered irregular forces ill-disciplined and too expensive to maintain. Having offered his services to both sides during the American War of Independence, he was engaged by General Howe, but his locally recruited Rangers were once again considered by regular British officers to be ill-disciplined, and they made little contribution to the war. Rogers was to die in obscurity in England in 1800, though his legacy lives on today in the American and British Special Forces.

The ground over which the American War of Independence was fought was very different from that to which the British Army had become accustomed when it campaigned in the Low Countries during the Seven Years War. The thirteen American colonies measured roughly 1,700 miles north to south and about 300 miles east to west. The many forests, rivers and mountains that covered the land meant that communications could be extremely slow, though not impossible. Indeed, lightly equipped troops could move with surprising speed through the forests, especially if accompanied by Indian guides. Even heavy equipment could be moved across country within a short period of time during the winter when rivers and marshes were frozen. This was well demonstrated by the American rebels when they moved all the heavy British guns and mortars captured at Crown Point and Fort Ticonderoga on Lake Champlain to Boston between November and February, where their employment caused Howe to abandon the British garrison.

Contemporary French maps also show that a fairly extensive system of roads already existed in North America by the start of the American War of Independence – even in the remote areas of north New York, where the first stages of the war were to be fought. The colonies by then had a population of over 3 million, of whom half a million were black slaves – though most people lived within 75 miles of the coastline. With settlers increasingly spreading towards the west, there was a need for not only communications to support agriculture, but also limited industrialization, which was beginning to take place both in large cities, such as New York and Charleston, and in the countryside. Goods had to be moved to markets, forges and mills had to be built, and there was a growing demand for locally manufactured agricultural implements.

As a young man George Washington had been employed as a surveyor by one of the greatest landowners in North America, Lord Fairfax, who owned 5 million acres between the Potomac and Rappahannock rivers. He wanted to survey his western boundaries and he chose the young Washington to help in this enormous task between 1748 and 1751. Washington's frequent journeys over the Allegheny Mountains gave him not only knowledge of that wild unspoilt terrain, but also an understanding of Indian life. Over the years he became much attracted to the beauty of the landscape and, when commander-in-chief, he claimed that if he ever needed to escape the British Army, all he had to do was take the Continental Army west where the British would not be able to find him. He was confident that he knew the country, and that the British did not.

During the American War of Independence, the British Army suffered greatly from lack of good generalship and confused strategic direction. The British government saw the war as being a limited local uprising that could be easily crushed by the superiority of regular troops and the occupation of major cities and ports along the eastern coastline of North America. Generals, such as Sir Henry Clinton, argued that the way to beat the rebels was through possession of Canada, New York and Chesapeake Bay and by naval blockade of the coastline. Such an approach would deny the rebellious colonists access to raw materials and ultimately force them to accept British rule.

However, such a strategy would take a long time to be successful – and time was not on the side of the British. Nor was North America ever likely to become the highest priority for the British Navy under the administration of Lord Sandwich, for his main task remained safeguarding Britain and its trading routes and stations. The British were therefore never prepared to deploy enough ships to North America to prevent the supply of munitions being sent from Europe to George Washington's army or to stop the French fleet from establishing temporary naval superiority on the eastern seaboard of America. As a result, the major British garrisons in North America – all of which were on the coast – became vulnerable to simultaneous attack from the sea by the French fleet and from the land by the American insurgents. It was such an attack that brought about the defeat at Yorktown and the loss of the American colonies. The attempt to maintain control of cities like New York and Charleston also required large numbers of British troops who, because they lacked sufficient numbers to sustain an offensive campaign, remained for most of the war in a state of siege by the insurgents. The lack of ground forces meant that the British never had the ability to manoeuvre at will throughout the colonies and this gave the initiative to the enemy. At the start of an insurgency war, time is not usually on the side of the insurgents. By the end of such wars, it is rarely on the side of the government. This was certainly true for the British at the end of the American War of Independence, and it has also proved to be true of the US-led occupation of Iraq.

In the spring of 2003, following the fall of Saddam Hussein, a fatal power vacuum had been created in Iraq that the insurgents and remnants of the Ba'athist regime were quick to fill. The immediate loss of control that led to widespread looting in Baghdad and other major Iraqi cities, the dismantlement of the Iraqi administration and the lack of political progress all convinced the Iraqis that the occupation force was far too weak to guarantee their future security. Paul Wolfowitz, one of the main architects of the forward strategy in the war against global terrorism before the conflict, had stated that the principal objective of the US forces in Iraq was 'to convince the Iraqi people that they no longer have to be afraid of Saddam. And once that happens I think that what you're going to find, and this is very important, you're going to find Iraqis out cheering American troops.' It was not so much Saddam Hussein that the Iraqis feared, but the ensuing breakdown of law and order in their country. As the ancient Iraqi proverb puts it, 'A hundred years of tyranny is better than one year of anarchy.'

Nevertheless, it took a considerable while for the American administration to realize that a long-term approach to nation-building in Iraq was needed, one that was very different from warfighting. The troops who had fought the war, many of whom were Reserve and National Guard units, expected to return home within a month or two of victory being declared. In fact, most of them remained in Iraq for a further year, by which time they were losing their commitment and positive attitudes.

It would have been far more difficult for the insurgency to take hold in Iraq if adequate security had been established and effective administration maintained by the Coalition forces immediately following the collapse of Saddam Hussein's regime. After all, the Iraqi bureaucracy was still functioning, and the army and police were still in existence, even if most of them had taken off their uniforms and gone home. They may have been inefficient and corrupt, but in the short term they were perfectly capable of preventing the anarchy that arose in Iraq following the invasion. What the Iraq administration lacked was proper direction. Furthermore, insufficient attention was given by the Coalition forces to the guarding of the critical infrastructure of the country and this was soon looted or broke down. Utilities stopped working and hospitals and schools ceased functioning. Salaries stopped being paid and criminal gangs started to operate. As a result of inaction by the Coalition forces, there followed a rapid and complete breakdown of law and order in Iraq and ultimately the disintegration of civil authority.

The cause of this was an astonishing failure of the strategic decision-making process in Washington. Even after the invasion of Iraq had actually begun in March 2003, General Jay Garner, the chief administrator in Iraq, still had not received clear political instructions from Washington regarding the strategy that was to be followed by the occupying forces. Indeed, the debate was continuing in Washington between the Pentagon and the State Department as to whether the occupation would be of short duration, sufficient only for the de-Ba'athification of the Iraq government and security forces, or whether the objective of the occupation forces was to impose democracy and order in Iraq. This would require a long-term American military presence in Iraq, in order to achieve the reconstruction of its economy and industry. Secretary of Defense Donald Rumsfeld was vigorously opposed to such a presence. In the end this policy was adopted, but too late and without sufficient manpower being committed to allow it to succeed.

Rumsfeld had rejected the original operational plan for the invasion of Iraq, codenamed OPLAN 1003–98. It had been drawn up by General Tony Zinni, the head of Central Command (CENTCOM), which is the US command responsible for the Middle East theatre of operations. He had assessed that it would take at least 380,000 American soldiers backed by their allies to provide sufficient security in Iraq in the aftermath of an invasion. The total strength of the occupying forces would therefore be 400,000 men. CENTCOM was clear that more troops would be needed for the post-conflict phase than for the actual invasion. For without such force levels it would be impossible to seal the borders of Iraq, establish law and order in all the major cities, dominate the countryside, eliminate any remaining resistance to the occupation, and finally locate and destroy the weapons of mass destruction (WMD) that were thought to exist in Iraq. This latter task was given the highest priority by US and British politicians. They had, of course, gone to war on the basis that Saddam Hussein possessed such weapons and their reputations were by now very much at stake. So great were their anxiety and determination to find weapons of mass destruction that the Coalition Special

Forces were diverted from their prime mission of capturing the remnants of Saddam Hussein's regime and told instead to search for the missing weapons. Once again, time and opportunities were lost because of political interference.

In spite of warnings to the contrary from many sources, throughout the planning process for the war Rumsfeld continued to insist that a large-scale invasion force was wholly unnecessary. Zinni's successor, General Tommy Franks, therefore had to settle for a force of 250,000 men, and even that force level would be soon reduced once Saddam Hussein was removed from power. The American administration firmly believed that the Iraqi people would welcome their liberators and that after the invasion there would be no need for a large stabilization force. The administration even rejected a plan to deploy 5,000 law enforcement officers to help with the maintenance of law and order. Yet there were no shortages of warnings about what would happen if civil authority in Iraq was not immediately established post-conflict from both within the US and abroad.

The administration's misjudgement of the true situation in Iraq was given embarrassing international visibility when on 1 May 2003, just over a month after the fall of Baghdad, President Bush stood proudly on board the USS *Lincoln* before a banner stating 'Mission Accomplished'. A month or so later he told American troops in Qatar, 'America sent you on a mission to remove a grave threat and to liberate an oppressed people, and that mission has been accomplished.' The war in Iraq was, in fact, only just beginning.

Another problem was created by the decision in Washington to put the Pentagon in charge of the reconstruction of Iraq. Soldiers, even when subordinate to the civil authority, are not the best people to undertake the complex business of nation-building – although in

45

counter-insurgency campaigns they may be a principal component involved. They simply do not have the civil experience or skills to govern. This is not surprising, as soldiers are principally trained for war. As John Adams, the second US president, said, 'soldiers make poor policemen. Where you deploy a platoon to quell one mob, you soon are faced by two mobs.' How true this is of Iraq.

In North America, during the latter part of the eighteenth century, the British administration had similarly failed to understand the nature of the war on which they were about to embark. They made the same mistake as the Bush administration in what was called at the time, 'blinking facts' – formulating strategy based on what they wanted to happen rather than on the harsh realities on the ground. Had the British immediately sent a large number of troops to North America when the insurgency first started, they would probably have been able to deny the insurgents the support of the people – even radical colonists like Samuel Adams would have been forced to accept the inevitability of British rule. But when General Gage asked for 32,000 troops to pacify New England, he was sent less than a quarter of that number. The British Army was simply too small to be able to defend its global Empire and at the same time fight an insurgency war in North America. In 1775 it numbered only 33,000 troops, some of whom were invalids. Hiring foreign mercenary troops was the only solution available to the British government. After an approach to Russia to send troops was turned down, negotiations were opened with the German states of Hesse-Cassel and Bruns-wick. In January 1776 it was agreed that these states should between them furnish 18,000 German regular troops who were well trained in European warfare. Although their arrival temporarily resolved the urgent problem of troop shortages, like British soldiers, the Germans were unsuited to insurgency warfare in America.

Therefore, as with the Americans in Iraq more than two centuries later, at no stage during the American War of Independence were the British ever able to deploy adequate numbers of troops to allow them to carry out their critically important tasks, which included holding the coastal belt and cities, maintaining control of the hinterland, and hunting down and destroying the rebels. It was necessary to carry out these tasks simultaneously in order to mobilize the support of the colonial population of North America, without which victory could not be won. By 1780, some 10,000 loyalists were fighting on the British side in North America, but after it became apparent that the British could not safeguard them or their families, their numbers rapidly dwindled. If sufficient security does not exist, then people will look to others or form into their own armed groups to defend themselves.

The inevitable result of continuing confusion between London and New York about how to fight the war in North America meant that none of the critical elements that were required for success were for long in place. Therefore, in spite of the fact that the British Army won more battles against the rebels than vice versa, the war itself was decisively lost. It had dragged on to a point where costs had become unaffordable, support at home had evaporated, and the alliance between France and the American rebels meant victory was no longer possible. What had been a locally contained colonial war had turned into a global one in which the French, Spanish and Dutch ships of the line ultimately outnumbered the British fleet. Not for two hundred years had British political isolation in Europe been so great or England been so threatened.

Yet possession of the American colonies had never been vitally important to any British imperial strategy. Keeping control of Canada, maintaining trading posts in the West Indies, holding on to Gibraltar, and increasing the British presence in the Indian subcontinent, were strategically far more important to the future economic wellbeing of the nation than retaining the thirteen North American colonies. Since 1763, the average yearly cost of £390,000 needed to provide for the defence of these colonies had taken up 4 per cent of the entire British national budget. This enormous sum by the standards of the eighteenth century had already been deemed unaffordable and had led to the passing of the unpopular Townsend duties of 1768 and Stamp Act of 1765 in an attempt to recoup some of the expenses. Nevertheless, the considerable cost of maintaining a peacetime garrison in North America was, of course, soon to be dwarfed by the huge expenditure needed to conduct a war at long distance, where virtually everything, including horse fodder, had to be shipped across the Atlantic.

Wars tend to be won or lost on the ground, as much by the comparative weaknesses and strengths of the military leaders as by those of the opposing armies. Britain was not fortunate in this respect, lacking at that time the quality of generals such as Marlborough, Wellington or Clive. While not being unpatriotic, the British generals of the Revolutionary War lacked the commitment and skills needed to fight a protracted counter-insurgency war.

Major General Thomas Gage, commander-in-chief in 1775 at the start of the American War of Independence, was a military bureaucrat and a soldier of limited fighting experience. As the second son of a viscount, he entered the army, serving for much of the time on the staff of his patron the Earl of Albemarle. On gaining command of his regiment, the 44th of Foot, he had taken part in the disastrous attempt by General Braddock to drive the French out of the Ohio Valley in 1755. Indeed, he had been in command of the advance party whose rout had caused such panic and retreat. Avoiding personal blame for the defeat, he raised a regiment of light infantry in 1755 called the 60th Royal American Regiment, which today still forms part of the British Army, and took part in the unsuccessful attempt to drive the French from Ticonderoga. Shortly afterwards he was given the mission to capture a French fort at La Galette at the head of the St Lawrence River, but once again he failed to accomplish his tasks. His commander-in-chief, Lord Amherst, wrote that Gage 'had found out difficulties where there were none'. However, his social connections ensured that once again he gained preferment. He was made governor of Montreal and promoted major general in 1761. After Amherst had been recalled following an Indian uprising in North America, Thomas Gage replaced him as commander-in-chief – a post that he was to occupy until he was himself recalled after the British defeats of Concord and Lexington and the bloody victory at Bunker and Breed's Hill in 1775. During this battle more than two-fifths of the British troops engaged were either killed or wounded, and one observer later commented that 'with many more victories such as that, the rebels would certainly win the war'. Thomas Gage had set out the initial pieces on the board for both sides in the American War of Independence and started a process that was to end in defeat for the Crown.

His successor was William Howe, 5th Viscount Howe, the British commander-in-chief in North America between 1775 and 1778. Howe was no stranger to war or North America and proved to be a far better soldier than any other senior commander on the British side. In 1757, he commanded the 58th Regiment at the capture of Louisburg and during Wolfe's expedition to Quebec he further distinguished himself at the head of a composite light battalion. He became adjutant general of the force that besieged and subsequently took Havana in 1762. By the close of the Seven Years War, he had gained the reputation of being one of the most brilliant young officers in the British Army. In 1774, he was made responsible for the training of light infantry companies and this experience should have given him an understanding of the need to employ these forces as independent manoeuvre groups when fighting against insurgents. However, he never employed them in this way during his time in command in North America. He also believed that to prosecute the war too firmly against the American rebels would preclude any future peace negotiations, failing to realize that the moment for compromise had ended with the Declaration of Independence. Although he was to win all his battles against the rebels, he failed to follow up each success, and thereby lost momentum. Had he destroyed the remnants of George Washington's insurgent army during the cold winter of 1776, when it numbered no more than 1,500 starving men, then the British would undoubtedly have won the war. It was an opportunity for victory that was not to be repeated. In 1778, he resigned his command, believing that the government at home had not given him the support, either political or material, that he deserved.

He was succeeded by General Henry Clinton, who also had experience of the North American colonies. He was the son of George Clinton, a governor of Newfoundland and New York, and had served in the New York militia as a lieutenant. He fought in the Seven Years War as an aide-de-camp to Prince Charles of Brunswick. At the battle of Freiberg in 1762, Prince Charles's army had been defeated by the allies, and Lieutenant Colonel Clinton, having been wounded, had been 'hacked by an ignorant German surgeon'. However, a reputation for gallantry had been established and after being promoted colonel and put in charge of the garrison in Gibraltar, he became a major general in 1772. He took part in the battles of Bunker Hill and Long Island in 1775 and subsequently became the commander of the British forces based in New York. After the British defeat at Saratoga he succeeded Howe as commander-in-chief in North America. As a tactician he was skilful and courageous, but he was never able to grasp the major strategic issues that needed to be resolved if the rebellion was to be defeated. He lacked self-esteem and tended to surround himself with flatterers and sycophants. He developed a reputation for being quarrelsome and quick-tempered and he fell out with most of his subordinate senior commanders – most fatally with Cornwallis. Importantly, he made little effort to support the American loyalists, on whom overall success in the American War of Independence so greatly depended.

The last of the three key British generals who arrived in America in 1775 to reinforce the British chain of command was Major General Johnny Burgoyne. He was entirely different in character from Clinton. A gambler and playwright, as well as a social climber, he possessed an overwhelming belief in his own ability. He had won distinction in Portugal during the Seven Years War and was now determined to personally bring about the defeat of the American uprising. Having convinced George III that it was possible to crush the rebellion by marching south from Canada and joining up with Howe's forces in New York, he led a disastrous expeditionary force into the Hudson Valley. Running short of supplies and faced by numerically superior American forces, he was finally forced to surrender his army to the rebels. His fall from grace was short-lived and he was soon promoted to be commander-in-chief in Ireland. Once again, he suffered, as had all the British generals, from a lack of strategic vision.

Lord Cornwallis, the general who in 1781 surrendered the British Army at Yorktown to Washington, thereby losing the American colonies, was a landowning aristocrat who was well connected in Court circles, having been an aide-de-camp to the King. Although opposed to the British policy in North America, he nevertheless felt it his duty to accompany his regiment when it was sent to open up a southern front against the rebels in the spring of 1776. By 1780, he had been given command of the British forces in South Carolina, and in 1781 he defeated General Nathanael Greene at Guilford Court House. However, his army shortly after ran out of supplies and he was forced to retreat. Having failed to pacify the Carolinas, he moved, without Clinton's authority, to Chesapeake Bay, from where he felt he would be able to relaunch his southern campaign. Here he was besieged at Yorktown by the French and American armies, now supported by a French fleet. He capitulated on 19 October 1781, so ending any British hope of victory. As with Burgoyne, surrender seemed not to carry the disgrace it deserved, and he was appointed Governor-General of India and commander-in-chief in Bengal. He was a competent field commander but one who failed to see the disastrous strategic consequences of taking his army north into Virginia.

If the British generals who were to command in North America left much to be desired, so did the state of the British Army. In 1775, there were some 7,000 soldiers in North America under command of General Gage, but these were dispersed throughout the colonies and along the western frontier. As a result the soldiers' training had suffered. Many of them were also rather elderly – they were men who had asked to remain in America for domestic reasons when their regiments had returned to England and had now settled into a new life in the colonies.

Reinforcements sent out from England were often composite battalions made up of soldiers from different regiments. A Guards battalion of one thousand that left England in March 1776, having been reviewed on Wimbledon Common by the King accompanied by the Duke of Wirtemberg, was actually made up of fifteen men drawn from each of the sixty-four companies that comprised the three Guards regiments. The commanding officer, Colonel Edward Mathew of the Coldstream Guards, and his officers and non-commissioned officers were posted in from different parts of the Brigade of Guards. Brigade Orders of 12 March state that 'His Majesty has been pleased to permit the officers of this detachment to make up an uniform with white lace . . . the serjeants to have their coats laced with white lace instead of gold, and the coats to be cut according to the pattern to be seen in the Orderly room of the Coldstream Regiment.' The officers and sergeants were also ordered to put aside their 'spontoons and halberds' and to be armed with 'fusees'. Only the last instruction would have been at all useful to men who were about to fight a war in hostile terrain 3,000 miles away.

The shortfalls in the US Army's preparation in Iraq are similar to those of the British in the American War of Independence. When confronted by the chaos of what has become a fully fledged insurgency war, US soldiers inevitably have fallen back on tried and tested warfighting tactics and used excessive military force in what was supposed to be a nation-building task. Because of the danger from suicide bombers and improvised explosive devices, American troops in Iraq have been forced to patrol in armoured vehicles and tend to open fire on any person or vehicle that approaches too closely. Therefore, they are compelled to live in secure military compounds and are unable to mix freely with local people. They have been manoeuvred into a classic situation of isolation by the insurgents, whose presence is universal.

Today, in Iraq, the people have become alienated from not only the occupying power, but also their own government. They believe that their politicians are corrupt or influenced by different sectarian factions. They do not believe that the government will ever be able to achieve the necessary levels of security in Iraq, or good governance, or even deliver the basic necessities of life such as electricity, water or sewage disposal. Since most Iraqis realize that the foreign occupiers will not remain in Iraq for ever, they know that ultimately there will be a struggle for political power between the Kurds, Sunnis and Shia. As a result of the weakness of the Iraqi government, all sides are fighting to gain control of the instruments of power in Iraq, making civil war ever more likely.

Although many Iraqis have joined the security forces, this does not imply that their ultimate loyalty lies with the Americans. It will lie with those who control their territory for most of the time, and currently these are the insurgent militia groups. Even the British, who were deployed into a far more benign environment in the southern provinces than the Americans further north, faced such a high level of threat from the insurgents that they too became disengaged from the Iraqi people. The police forces that the British Army has spent four years training are now entirely controlled by two separate Iranian-backed militias. Isolation from the mass of the people cost the British the war in North America, and it is likely to do the same for the Coalition forces in Iraq.

Chapter Two

In general, our generals were outgeneralled.

JOHN ADAMS

On 18 April 1775, a small British force was sent out from Boston by General Gage, the British commander-in-chief in America, with instructions to seize and destroy the ammunition depot at Concord, in order to prevent it falling into the hands of the Massachusetts militia. On the way, the advance party commanded by Major Pitcairn met a number of colonial militiamen drilling on the village green at Lexington. When he ordered them to disperse, a number of shots were fired at him, one wounding his horse. The British troops returned fire, killing eight Americans including their commanding officer, Captain John Parker, and wounding several others. These were the opening shots of a war that was to last eight long years.

Although they succeeded in accomplishing their mission, the British troops were later halted by a hastily formed group of rebels, led by a local farmer, on a bridge near Concord. The Massachusetts provincial congress had long since planned what to do in the event of an attack by the British troops based in Boston. It had arranged to mobilize the minute companies, so called because they were on immediate standby, as well as the regiments of the provincial militia. Their numbers totalled 7,000 men. There was even a primitive command and control system in place to conduct operations. It was no surprise, therefore, that in the subsequent retreat to Boston the British lost 73 killed and 174 wounded to the American militia, who had been greatly angered by the slaughter at Lexington. The expeditionary force was only saved from complete annihilation by the arrival of reinforcements from Boston, which included artillery. Lacking critical intelligence about their enemy, the British had greatly misjudged the nature of the operation. It had been a disastrous start to the war. The same cannot be said for the US forces who invaded Iraq. Their difficulties arose when the military successes had ended.

Fired by this unexpected success, thousands of New Englanders rallied to the rebel cause and thus began the long, drawn-out siege of the British forces in Boston. In response to these rebellious incidents, 7,000 men were sent from England to reinforce the garrison in Boston, break the siege and crush the rebellion. It was less than a quarter of the number requested by General Gage, but the British government still insisted that only a few troops would be needed to defeat the rebels. With the troops came a letter from the Secretary of State for the Colonies, Lord Dartmouth, stating, 'By the time this letter reaches you, the army under your command will be equal to any operation that may be necessary.' The same bland assessment was, of course, made by Secretary of Defense Rumsfeld to his generals almost exactly 228 years later.

On the American side, on 10 May 1775 a second Congress was convened in Philadelphia, which resolved to put the colonies into a state of defence. It authorized the raising of an army of 13,600 men, the construction of forts and the issue of arms, equipment and provisions to the militia. These were to be paid for by the issue of 3 million dollar notes inscribed 'The United Colonies'. On 15 June 1775, another momentous decision was taken that was to have far-reaching effects on the outcome of the war – the appointment of George Washington as commander-in-chief of the Continental Army, probably the only American who had the tenacity and leadership to see the rebellion through to victory. Washington was well over six feet tall, with a strong physique, and was also a gifted horseman, so looked every inch a military commander. He was to be supported by four major generals and eight brigadier generals who, like him, lacked experience in commanding large formations. But they had an unswerving belief in the justice of their cause – something that was conspicuously lacking in the more experienced British generals they were about to confront.

A feeling of excitement mixed with foreboding spread amongst the colonists as news of the decisions taken by Congress spread. The die had been cast, but people knew that civil war was the most terrible of all forms of combat. At the outset, roughly one-third of the population supported the rebels, one-third remained neutral and one-third were loyal to the Crown. When the war ended in 1783, the American population had split into two camps with the majority siding with the rebellion – if only because they did not wish to suffer the political, social or economic consequences of being on the losing British side. What had begun as a small rebellion turned into a civil war because the British were never able to exercise sufficient control in the thirteen colonies and therefore could not persuade the majority of Americans to support established British rule.

This is a pattern typical of the development of most insurgencies in history. In the beginning a few determined extremists, who are prepared to take life and sacrifice their own for their beliefs, inevitably start at a disadvantage. The governing authority usually responds to their isolated attacks with oppressive measures in an attempt to arrest or kill the rebels and their supporters. Government forces then engage in wide-scale search and destroy operations that result in the alienation of the population, most of whom were probably not committed to either side at the start of the insurrection. Because the government is unlikely to be able to defend the civilians from intimidation and attack by the insurgents, ultimately people are forced to side with the rebels. Those who can instil the most fear in the population exercise the most leverage.

This has been as much the pattern for the war in Iraq as it was for the British during the American War of Independence. The original Coalition objectives of creating in Iraq an enduring democratic state, good governance and security became realistically unachievable in the face of high levels of sectarian conflict, widespread corruption and lack of progress in civil reconstruction that exist in the country today.

The first problem that Washington faced as rebel commander-in-chief was to impose some form of strategic coherence on the rebellion that was rapidly spreading throughout the colonies of New England. He needed to develop a campaign plan that would give him sufficient time to build up his military resources. Clearly, he had to avoid decisive military defeat, but at the same time he had to prevent the British from imposing control over the civilian population, thereby ensuring their continuing support. This latter requirement was a key objective in his campaign plan, and to achieve it he would use the militia. Although he instinctively disliked the ill discipline and unreliability that were the militia's principal characteristics, he saw that only it could provide a permanent rebel presence on the ground. It would be the militia's responsibility to harass the British, and protect the centres of rebellion and key ports through which essential supplies from the rebels' allies overseas, mainly the French, could be delivered to the rebels. When needed, the militia could also be called upon to concentrate its forces to combine with the Continental Army in set-piece attacks against the British. Writing to the governor of Connecticut in the summer of 1775, Washington clearly set out his future military doctrine: 'I wish I could extend protection to all, but the numerous detachments necessary to remedy the evil would amount to dissolution of the army.' The Continental Army would be reserved for decisive action against the British, not distributed in small packets around the country on protection duties.

He was able to see that the British would never have sufficient numbers of troops to allow them to hunt down and destroy the Continental Army, provide a permanent credible military presence throughout the colonies, and at the same time defend their main bases. Wherever the British were absent or too weak on the ground, the uncommitted elements in the American colonial population would be compelled to give their support to the rebellion by the ever-present patriot militia. This would be achieved through a mixture of violence, intimidation and occasional appeals to the American spirit of independence. Washington, of course, did not directly command the state militias, whose authority derived from the state legislature, and he often found himself in competition with them for recruits. However, he depended on them to provide a rebel presence throughout the colonies that would disperse the British effort. He also relied heavily on the state militias whenever the Continental Army engaged the British in set-piece battles.

The imperatives facing Bush and Rumsfeld in Iraq today are very similar to those that confronted the British in

North America, and it is surprising that they have not allowed the lessons of their own Revolutionary War to shape their modern strategic approach to the war in Iraq. For the US-led forces in Iraq had the same priority tactical-level tasks to perform if they were to succeed in their strategic goals. These tasks included establishing immediate law and order throughout the country, hunting down the remnants of the Ba'athist regime, closing the porous borders between Iraq, Syria and Iran, and finally setting about the reconstruction and administration of the country. All these tasks were interrelated and therefore had to be achieved simultaneously. Yet, as has been already pointed out, there were simply too few troops to adequately carry out even the first of these tasks in Iraq. The result has been chaos, a steady loss of control and the creation of an insurgency that within four years took Iraq to the brink of civil war. The US administration had simply ignored the classic dilemma of all counter-insurgency wars.

By nature, Washington would have liked to follow a conventional military strategy aimed at the decisive defeat of the British Army in fixed battle. But after Washington had been severely defeated by the British in New York in 1776 and at Brandywine and Germantown in 1777, he finally understood that set-piece battles against a better trained and equipped army would usually end in disaster for his newly formed Continental Army. Only when he felt that the balance of force was in the Americans' favour – as it was at Saratoga – did he permit the Continental Army, massively reinforced by state militias, to confront regular British troops. As he wrote at the time, 'We should on all occasions avoid a general action, nor put anything to the risk unless compelled by a necessity into which we ought never to be drawn.'

Thus, the American strategy would consist of attacking the

enemy supply lines, eliminating loyalist support within the population and buying time for the entry of allies into the war on its side. This was called the War of Posts or the Fabian option, after the Roman general Fabius Cunctator, who, although less operationally skilled than Hannibal, defeated him by retreating whenever Hannibal and his Carthaginian army attacked and attacking whenever they retreated. If all else failed, Washington knew that he could withdraw his army to the west over the Allegheny Mountains where he would be out of the reach of the British and from where he would be able to relaunch the rebellion.

As he travelled north from Philadelphia in 1775 to take up his command, Washington had been much encouraged by news of the outcome of the battle of Bunker Hill, which had taken place on 17 June, two days after his appointment as commander-in-chief. Though a technical defeat for the Americans, who had been forced to retreat from two key features on the north side of Boston – Bunker Hill and Breed's Hill – terrible losses had been inflicted on the British troops. But the newly arrived British regular troops commanded by General Howe had not ultimately been able to break the siege or destroy the rebel militia army. This failure to turn a tactical success into a strategic advantage was to become a common British characteristic of the war, and Washington was able to declare, with some credibility, that after this battle 'the liberties of the country are safe'.

Having pinned down the British Army in Boston, Washington mistakenly decided to move onto the attack and gave his permission for the invasion of Canada, believing that the American rebels were strategically well positioned to achieve this. Washington knew that the British garrison in Canada was relatively weak, and he also believed that a significant number of Canadians would support the American move to throw off British rule. He was quite wrong about this latter point. It is also a mistake for any insurgent force to take on regular government troops too early in a campaign.

Nevertheless, he had been encouraged in his plan by the fact that earlier that year, on 10 May 1775, two important positions on Lake Champlain – Fort Ticonderoga and Crown Point – had been taken by the rebels. These forts had originally been built by the French to defend their Canadian possessions from the English colonies in New England, but after the withdrawal of the French from Canada they had lost their strategic significance. But with rebellion now breaking out in New England they once again became important, for they blocked the way of any invading force from Canada, and it was widely known that the British were planning such a move. The seizure of the forts had been accomplished by a Vermont frontiersman, Ethan Allen, and a group of rebels called the Green Mountain Boys who had joined forces with Benedict Arnold and a company of Connecticut Guards. Subverting the small British garrison, which had not been told that a rebellion had broken out, they overwhelmed it without loss on either side. The capture of this fort had not only secured the rebels' northern flank, but also given a firm start line from which to launch attacks against the British garrisons in Montreal and Quebec.

On hearing of the capture of the two forts, Washington appointed Major General Philip Schuyler – one of the four major generals of the new Continental Army – to command an expeditionary force with instructions to invade Canada. Philip Schuyler came from one of the wealthiest and most influential families in the colony of New York and had also been a delegate at the second Continental Congress of May 1775. A veteran of the Seven Years War, he had fought over much of the territory in the upper parts of the colony – the very ground that would first have to be secured if there was to be an invasion of Canada. Schuyler decided to despatch two armies into Canada, one from Lake Champlain against Montreal, led by Brigadier General Richard Montgomery, and the other against Quebec, led by Benedict Arnold. The latter was to be launched directly from Maine, moving first up the Kennebec River and then crossing the watershed of the Appalachian Mountains, following the Chaudiere River down to Quebec.

The operation was not a success, although Montgomery was able to take Montreal on 12 November 1775 without difficulty. However, General Guy Carleton, the British governor of Canada, who had been warned that the American rebels intended to invade Canada, had deliberately given up Montreal and concentrated his forces in Quebec. Meanwhile, Arnold's small army had been greatly weakened by the difficult approach march across country into Canada and was unable to mount an independent attack. It was therefore compelled to wait for reinforcements from Montgomery. The delay proved costly, for by the time the rebels did finally attack on 31 December 1775, Carleton had greatly strengthened his defences. The rebels were easily defeated and their commander, Montgomery, was killed. The remnants of the invading army were now reduced to some 350 volunteers, who continued an ineffective siege of the city until the spring of 1776, when the British mounted a counter-offensive. This forced the American expeditionary force to retreat southwards, abandoning its positions at the northern end of Lake Champlain and retiring to Ticonderoga.

However, Benedict Arnold was determined to halt the British advance and he started building a naval flotilla of sixteen vessels mounting seventy guns on Lake Champlain. The work was completed in September 1776. Meanwhile, the British had already started work on establishing their own fleet, and Carleton had dismantled three Royal Naval ships and rebuilt them at St John's on Lake Champlain. These ships were supported by twenty smaller gunboats and 400 small troop-carrying vessels. The work of constructing this fleet had greatly delayed the British advance and it was October before the British fleet, which heavily outgunned the rebels, was ready.

On 11 October 1776, lying in wait in side channels off Valcour Island some 50 miles north of Ticonderoga, Arnold allowed the British fleet to sail downwind of his ships before launching his attack. The British were consequently forced to tack back against the wind, which allowed the rebels to slip away to the south. However, the wind changed and the British were finally able to run down and destroy the rebel flotilla. It was later claimed that 'the naval efforts of a soldier had saved the American Revolution because of the delay inflicted on the British advance south'.

Fortunately for the Americans, Carleton's forces on shore had also found progress far more difficult than expected. Lieutenant John Enys of the 29th Worcestershire Regiment was part of the pursuing force and wrote of the country on 10 October 1776, 'It is impossible to conceive what a disagreeable March we suffered from this until daylight, our way laying through Swamps and broken ground with an eminence of fallen Trees over which we are continually falling as it was very dark. It was with the utmost difficulty that we could see the Man before us.'

Carleton had also been falsely informed that Ticonderoga was held by a force of 20,000 men. In fact, the garrison numbered no more than 5,000, as numbers had been greatly reduced by desertions and smallpox. Even if he had succeeded in taking Ticonderoga, Carleton could not rely on reaching New England before winter set in. He therefore decided to return to Canada, from where he would be able to launch a new offensive in the spring. The decision to withdraw nevertheless had a psychologically damaging effect on the loyalists in upper New York, who 'were all waiting with eager impatience for assistance'.

Thus, when the British did finally move to secure the line of the Hudson River a year later in 1777 and launched an offensive southward from Canada, they had already largely forfeited the support of the remaining loyalists. They also had to retake the fort of Ticonderoga at the southern end of Lake Champlain before moving on to take Fort Edward and Fort Anne in the Hudson River Valley, both of which had lain within their grasp the year before. Carleton's failure to secure a British presence on the upper reaches of the Hudson River in 1776 fatally undermined the chances of the British expeditionary force under Burgoyne succeeding in its goal of isolating the rebels of New England by taking control of the Hudson River. As Sir John Fortescue wrote over a hundred years later, 'Very different would it have been if the British had been commanded by such a man as Arnold whose amazing skill, gallantry, and resource make him undoubtedly the hero of this short campaign.'

From the American failure to take Canada Washington was to learn a lesson that all insurgents have to learn early on, which is that they must never fight on too many fronts simultaneously or send ill-equipped troops against a superior military force. Even today in Iraq, after their costly attempt to take on the might of the US armed forces in Fallujah in 2004 the insurgents have been careful not to engage the American forces in major set-piece battles. They have now adopted the classic indirect approach, which involves undermining political support for the occupation forces and Iraqi government and winning the local population over to their side.

While Montgomery and Arnold were fighting in Canada, the army that was besieging Boston needed Washington's urgent attention. The British forces in Boston numbered 8,000 men, supported by two regiments of marines as well as powerful artillery. At anchor in the bay, less than a mile away from the American positions, lay powerful ships of the Royal Navy. General Howe, the commander-in-chief, was an experienced general who had already shown his willingness to fight the rebels head on. Once he had been reinforced by the considerable numbers of troops that were finally on their way from England, a number of options would be open to him. He could renew his attempt to break the siege of Boston or attack the rebels at any point along the American coastline from the sea. Most worryingly from Washington's perspective, he could once again launch an offensive southwards from Canada along the line of the Hudson, so cutting off the New England colonies from the south. There was no time to lose in these early days if the flame of the American Revolution was not to be snuffed out.

On 2 July 1775, Washington arrived in the small town of Cambridge outside Boston where the headquarters of the besieging rebel army was located, and he immediately reorganized the army into three divisions. He gave command of the right wing to General Artemis Ward, who had until then commanded all the rebel forces around Boston. The left wing Washington gave to General Lee who, although he thought him 'fickle', was the most militarily experienced soldier amongst his senior officers. Washington gave the centre to General Putnam, who had fought with great distinction earlier that year at Bunker and Breed's Hill.

The next day – only a fortnight after being appointed commander-in-chief in Philadelphia – Washington issued a first General Order, calling for a complete inventory of the army positioned around Boston. This gave him some idea of the magnitude of the difficulties facing him. The army consisted of 16,600 men of whom 9,000 were from Massachusetts – a notoriously unruly body of men whose spirit of independence often took the form of outright insubordination. Many of the rebel soldiers had no proper uniforms and were short of ammunition, especially gunpowder. Discipline was difficult to exercise when so many officers had been elected into their rank by their own men, upon whom they were therefore reluctant to impose too firm a control. The army that he was to command was no more than 'a mixed multitude of people, under very little discipline, order or government'. In effect it was a typical insurgent force at the start of a rebellion. General Lee soon discovered that these deficiencies extended to combat support, where the situation was 'exactly the reverse of what had been represented. We were assured at Philadelphia that the army was stocked with engineers. We found not one. We were assured that we should find an expert train of artillery. They have not a single gunner and so on . . .'

Of even greater concern to Washington was the fact that most of the soldiers' period of service ended on 31 December 1775, after which there was a possibility that Washington would be left with no army at all. He desperately needed to raise a regular force of soldiers that could be supported by the militia. Only with long-term enlistments would the Continental Army develop the skills and discipline necessary to win the war. This had in principle been agreed by Congress, but the individual representatives of the thirteen colonies were suspicious of Washington's wish to create a regular army, which they believed could become a threat to their own independence. They were conscious of how, only just over a century before, Oliver Cromwell had built a New Model Army and used it to seize political power.

Nevertheless, in spite of the many political and physical difficulties facing him, Washington succeeded in 'disbanding one army and raising another'. By January 1776, Washington had managed to recruit 12,500 men as regulars and had succeeded in persuading 7,000 of the militia to stay on. He and his newly appointed generals were starting to impose their will on the ad hoc insurgent army. A military chaplain observing the frantic activity at the time wrote, 'There is a great overturning in the camp as to order and regularity. New lords, new laws. The Generals Washington and Lee are upon the lines every day. New orders from His Excellency are read to the respective regiments every morning after prayers. The strictest government is taking place and great distinction is made between officers and soldiers. Every one is made to know his place and keep it. Or be tied up and receive thirty or forty lashes according to his crime.'

To resolve the desperate shortages of supplies, Washington appointed Joseph Trumbull, the son of the governor of Connecticut, to the post of commissary general. At one point during the siege of Boston there had only been sufficient powder available for nine cartridges per man. Happily for the insurgents, the British remained ignorant of this fact. Washington also appointed his old wartime colleague Horatio Gates as adjutant general. Gates had fought alongside him under Braddock in the disastrous attempt to capture Fort Duquesne during the Seven Years War. He enjoyed an inflated military reputation and was subsequently to prove a poor commander in the field. Nevertheless, he was an excellent administrator and rapidly established a central system of military records, which helped to bring some uniformity to the different regiments that had come from the various colonies.

Apart from shortages of supplies, Washington still had insufficient funds with which to pay the soldiers or to make up the deficiencies that faced him everywhere. As he put it, 'I find myself already much embarrassed for want of a military chest', and his letters to Congress at this time became an endless pleading for money. Indeed, the rebel soldiers were on the point of mutiny because of lack of pay, and it was only when in June 1776 his friend and great supporter John Adams was appointed head of the Board of War and Ordnance that things started to improve. By the end of that year the period of enlistment for the Continental Army had been raised to three years.

Throughout the harsh winter months, a tactical impasse prevailed between the growing insurgent army and the British forces in Boston. Washington kept up pressure on the British by reinforcing his siege line and launching attacks against the British positions. The British replied by bombardment, but did not launch any major attacks. Still determined to win an early and decisive victory against the British, on 4 March 1776 Washington successfully launched an assault on Dorchester Heights – a dominating feature to the south of Boston harbour. Although it was only occupied by the rebels temporarily, the loss of this vital ground made it thereafter impossible for the British to hold on to Boston. When he saw the redoubts that the rebels had built, Howe exclaimed, 'The rebels have done more work in one night than my whole army would have done in a month.'

Washington also realized that the British positions could now be subjected to direct artillery fire from the heavy rebel guns that Henry Knox, a former Boston bookseller, had managed to bring down from Ticonderoga that winter. Two weeks later, General Howe, who clearly understood that the isolated British garrison in Boston served no useful strategic purpose, finally made the decision to evacuate Boston and establish his major operational base in New

York. Washington had gained his first tactical victory against the British.

Thus, after a year of inactivity, the centre of gravity of the war moved south to New York, where the British were about to despatch a vast invasion fleet consisting of 32,000 troops, including 8,000 well-trained Hessians. The transport of this army probably represented as great a feat of planning as the extraordinary achievement of the Americans two and a quarter centuries later when they moved an enormous force of men and material across the Atlantic in the opposite direction, prior to the start of the first Gulf War.

In 1776, the British force was to be shipped across the Atlantic in an armada of 170 troop-carrying vessels supported by ten ships of the line and twenty frigates. It was the largest fleet ever assembled by the British and it was an indication of their determination to suppress the uprising in the American colonies. Every item needed to maintain an army in hostile territory had to be shipped 3,000 miles across an ocean where sailing in winter was an extremely hazardous undertaking. Forage for the horses, tents for the soldiers, ammunition, muskets and guns as well as the 300 heavy wagons needed to transport them had to be gathered together in five different embarkation ports in England and despatched to America in accordance with a highly detailed timetable. However, storms and head winds made delay inevitable, and it was not until 3 July 1776 that the troops finally made their first landings on Staten Island.

But first the southern colonies had to be secured. The British general Clinton was ordered by Howe to lead an expeditionary force to establish a major British presence in the south. It was hoped that this presence would encourage an uprising amongst the numerous armed loyalists, most notably the Highlanders living in the mountains of North

Carolina. Unfortunately, bad weather delayed the passage of Clinton, as well as the naval reinforcements from Britain that were to support the expedition. Becoming impatient with the endless delays, the Highlanders moved far too early while Clinton was still afloat and therefore not in a position to support them. Commanded by an eighty-year-old veteran, Colonel McLeod, the Highlanders were comprehensively defeated at Moore's Bridge on 27 February 1776, losing 850 men killed or captured. This early rebel victory helped light the flame of revolutionary fervour in the south that the British Army under Cornwallis was never able to extinguish.

This premature uprising was mirrored in our own time when the Shia tribes in the south of Iraq rose up against Saddam Hussein after the first Gulf War, on the expectation that America and its allies would come to their aid. When this assistance failed to materialize, the Shia uprising was crushed with a great deal of brutality by forces loyal to Saddam Hussein. It is no wonder that the Shia population in Iraq so widely mistrusts the current American-led occupation force and now looks to Iran and its own militias for protection.

When the British fleet finally arrived in America, commanded by Sir Peter Parker, Clinton decided to attack Charleston. First it was necessary to destroy a small rebel garrison on Sullivan's Island, which protected the approaches to the Charleston River. Rather than mounting a frontal amphibious assault at the fort on the island, Clinton decided to land his force of 500 men on nearby Long Island, which was undefended. From there he planned an assault on foot across the narrow channel that separated the two islands, having been assured that the maximum depth of water at low tide was 18 inches. In fact, the actual depth of water made such a crossing impossible. However,

Clinton made no attempt to recover his force from Long Island and relaunch the attack from elsewhere.

Sir Peter Parker therefore decided to destroy the fort by naval gunfire. However, in this case, the approach channel to Sullivan's Island proved to be too shallow for the British ships and after an exchange of fire in which Parker lost one vessel and had four times as many casualties as the insurgents, the entire British force withdrew and sailed off to New York. The first British operation to gain control of the south had been a fiasco, not least because of great indecisiveness about where to land, the early failure to support the loyalists and a lack of coordination between Clinton and Parker. Such a lack of coordination between the army and the navy was to bedevil British operations throughout the entire war.

While the British were assembling their invasion force in England, Washington had not been inactive in North America. He had decided to deny New York to the British, a city whose strategic value he had identified – quite wrongly as it turned out – as being vital to the success of the rebellion. He also believed that New York City was a hotbed of British sympathizers who needed to be eliminated. This much was true. He arrived in New York in April and immediately started preparing its defence. He had still not understood that insurgents trying to hold ground against a superior military force would always be defeated. The city of New York, even in the eighteenth century, was in any case far too large for Washington's small army to control, and because of its position at the mouth of the Hudson River it could not be properly defended without naval superiority. And, of course, it was British, not American, ships that controlled the approaches to New York. Nevertheless, Washington persuaded Congress to support his plan, telling them, 'If our Troops will behave well, have everything to contend that Freemen hold dear, they (the British) will have to wade through much blood & slaughter before they can carry any part of our Works.'

As with many subsequent rebel commanders, his early revolutionary enthusiasm and rhetoric were to cloud his military judgement. Three centuries later, Washington's hubris was to be matched by Saddam Hussein's convictions that his Republican Guards and Fedayeen would be able to defeat the US invasion forces in the battle for Baghdad. In the same way that Howe had been able to manoeuvre his forces at will owing to his command of the maritime environment, during the invasion of Iraq air supremacy gave the American forces similar freedom of manoeuvre. As a result, Howe and General Franks were able to win relatively easy tactical level victories and occupy the capital cities of their respective foes. However neither military commander was subsequently able to turn his initial success into strategically decisive victories, for both Howe and Franks had mistakenly pursued territorial gain – and in Frank's case also regime change – instead of concentrating on the elimination of the enemy forces.

In the summer of 1776, Washington was forced to split his force into two separate elements in order to defend both Long Island and Manhattan. It was thus relatively easy for Howe to engage the American insurgent force piecemeal. Having mastery of the sea, Howe was able to concentrate his force and mount an attack wherever he chose. Nor did he make the mistake of underestimating the American resolve to stand and fight from their entrenched positions. He had already seen what Americans could do in Boston, even when only protected by hastily prepared defences. Seeing that Washington had positioned only a third of his troops on Brooklyn Heights, Howe realized that the insurgent left flank was open and therefore sent a force under

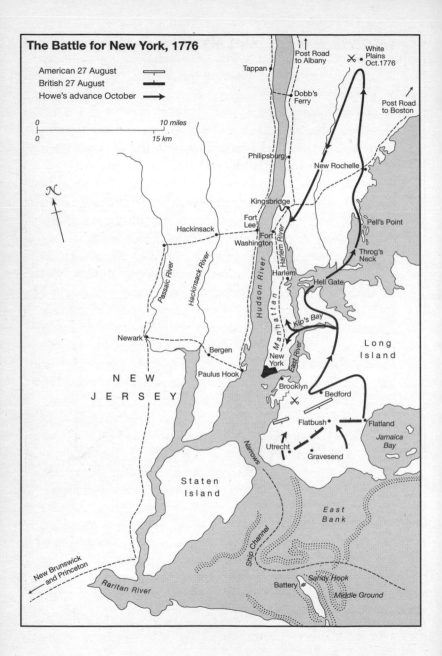

The Battle for New York, 1776

American 27 August
British 27 August
Howe's advance October

0   10 miles
0   15 km

N

Post Road to Albany

White Plains Oct.1776

Tappan

Dobb's Ferry

Post Road to Boston

Philipsburg

New Rochelle

Kingsbridge

Fort Lee

Pell's Point

Hackinsack

Fort Washington

Throg's Neck

Harlem

Hell Gate

Passaic River

Hackinsack River

Hudson River

Harlem River

Kip's Bay

Long Island

Newark

Bergen

New York

East River

Paulus Hook

Manhattan

Brooklyn

Bedford

NEW

Flatbush

Flatland

JERSEY

Utrecht

Gravesend

Jamaica Bay

Narrows

Staten Island

East Bank

Ship Channel

New Brunswick and Princeton

Raritan River

Battery

Sandy Hook

Middle Ground

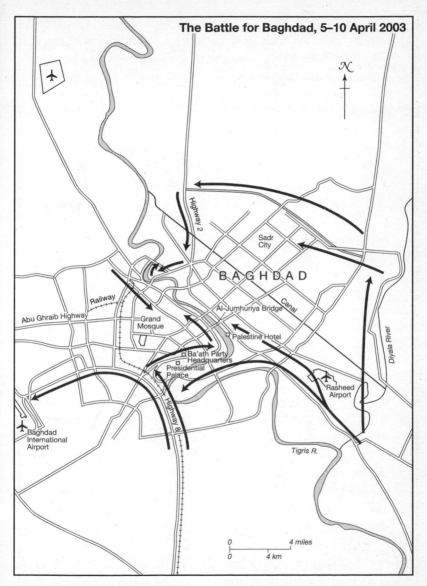

The Battle for Baghdad, 5–10 April 2003

In Baghdad, the main purpose of the operation was to drive the Iraqi Army and Fedayeen from the capital. The capture of the Iraqi leadership was a secondary priority. Howe made a similar error in allowing Washington to escape from New York.

Clinton to exploit this weakness. On 27 August 1776, the British launched their main attack, and within a short time they had captured the first line of trenches. On hearing this bad news, Washington hurried over from Manhattan to take command. Realizing that the situation was hopeless, he gave orders for the insurgent positions to be evacuated and the entire force withdrew that night from Long Island. The American losses had been 1,500 and the British, 300. It had been a massive defeat for Washington, but worse was to follow.

Although Howe did not immediately press forward on 13 September 1776, he subsequently landed troops on the south end of Manhattan, so forcing Washington to retreat north to Harlem. Then, bypassing Washington's forces on Manhattan, he disembarked a major force further north at Throg's Neck from where he was able to threaten Washington's entire army, which was now pinned between the Hudson and Harlem Rivers. Following a council of war on 16 October 1776, at which Lee recommended the withdrawal of the rebel forces from New York, Washington decided to evacuate Manhattan. He took his forces to the north of the city where he was determined to make a final stand against the British at White Plains. Tradition has it that Washington was only able to evacuate his 3,000 troops from Manhattan without loss because at a critical moment an American lady who sympathized with the insurgents had invited Howe to a lengthy lunch that she made sure lasted well into the afternoon. This so delayed the British advance that the insurgents just had time to escape.

When it did take place, the battle at White Plains once again proved indecisive and the Americans were forced to retreat further back into the surrounding hills. Washington had given overall responsibility to General Nathanael Greene for the defence of Fort Washington and Fort Lee, which lay on each side of the Hudson River. However, Greene was given only a vague instruction by Washington that he should not hazard the rebel troops, equipment and guns located in the fort on the east side of the river: 'I am therefore inclined to think it will not be prudent to hazard the men and stores at Mount Washington, but as you are on the spot leave it to you to give such orders as to evacuating Mount Washington.'

But Howe unexpectedly swung south back towards New York and in a surprise attack captured Fort Washington, taking 2,800 insurgent prisoners, as well as their equipment and guns. Washington's hold on New York had now become untenable. Three nights later, Howe launched an attack led by Cornwallis across the Hudson River on Fort Lee on the opposite bank. This time Greene was less optimistic about his chances of defeating the British and on hearing of their approach, fled with his remaining insurgent force.

In a short period of three months, Washington had been comprehensively defeated in a series of rolling engagements with the British. The insurgents had been unable to withstand the assaults of the redcoats and Hessians, and in the words of John Adams, 'in general, our generals were out-generalled'. Washington came in for a good deal of personal criticism, both in Congress and amongst his senior commanders. Lee wrote, 'Indecision bids fair for tumbling down the goodly fabric of American freedom and with it the rights of mankind. 'Twas indecision of Congress prevented our having a noble army and on an excellent footing. 'Twas indecision in our military councils which cost us Fort Washington.'

Washington had only survived because of the ineptitude of Howe, who had failed to block the escape route of the American forces through north Manhattan to Kingsbridge, from where they were able to cross the Hudson River.

Howe's plan instead consisted of phased attacks with the objectives of capturing New York and its important docks and port facilities. It was a conventional, somewhat ponderous plan which took nearly four months to complete, in spite of his superiority in numbers and his total mastery of the sea. The rebels were only of secondary interest to Howe, although of course they had incidentally to be driven from their positions if the British territorial objectives were to be seized. He had entirely ignored Clinton's original suggestion that the British should cut off and destroy the rebel army in Manhattan by moving directly up the Hudson River to Kingsbridge.

When the Americans planned to invade Iraq in 2003, Franks similarly failed to identify the true centre of gravity of the operation, codenamed Cobra II, which was to destroy Saddam Hussein's combat ability, including the Fedayeen, and prevent them from regrouping and starting a guerrilla campaign against the occupying forces. He was completely confident that the American forces could deal with the conventional troops of the Iraqi Army and this proved to be so, for in the words of the US land force commander Lieutenant General David McKiernan, the American forces were 'the finest team gathered anywhere in the world'. It was predicted that even the Special Republican Guard would melt away in the face of superior force. However, no action was undertaken by Franks to bring these forces back into being under the flag of the new Iraqi government, despite the fact that a Phase VI plan that dealt with the post conflict phase of Operation Iraq Freedom had been put together in Washington. This plan foresaw the need rapidly to establish control in Iraq in the immediate post war period, and this was to be done by sealing the borders of the country, protecting its critical national infrastructure and, most importantly, regrouping the Iraqi military. But given Rumsfeld's arbitrary limit on the size of the invasion force, the Phase VI plan also necessitated the drawing away of military forces from the main land component in order to accomplish these vital tasks which would have to be executed simultaneously with the land invasion. The plan therefore received little or no support from Franks, who seems to have considered his job done with the toppling of Saddam Hussein's statue in Baghdad. Therefore, just as Howe had let Washington's troops live to fight another day by slipping away across the Hudson River, so Franks let Saddam Hussein's conventional and irregular forces slip away into the backstreets and byways of Iraq, where people like Abu Musab al Zarqarwi were able to reform and begin an insurgency that has brought America to the brink of defeat, and the Iraqi people close to civil war.

By December 1776, the American insurgent army had been reduced to 5,000 men and it had lost much of its equipment and artillery, but Washington had nevertheless succeeded in breaking contact with the British. His rebel army was therefore able to withdraw to the west, across the Delaware River into Pennsylvania. On the way, his best general, Lee, who had instructions to delay the British pursuit, had been captured. Howe now occupied the whole of New Jersey, from where he was able to threaten the rebel capital, Philadelphia, across the Delaware River. It was an ignominious end to the year, which had started so well for Washington. He told his half-brother, 'I think the game is near up'. An English political commentator, Tom Paine, who supported the revolution wrote a pamphlet called *The Crisis* that began with the words: 'These are the times to try men's souls. The summer soldier and the sunshine patriot will, in this crisis, shrink from the service of their country.'

However, both Washington and Paine were being too

pessimistic. They did not allow for the inertia of Howe, who made no attempt to finally put an end to the rebellion by pursuing and destroying the remnants of Washington's army. Nor did Howe make allowances for the extraordinary resilience of the American revolutionaries, who by then had no other choice but to continue with the war. With an astonishingly rapid recovery of spirit among the rebellious colonists, 1,500 militiamen from Pennsylvania joined Washington, and Philip Schuyler sent a further 1,000 men from the north. At a time when the Americans were well-nigh defeated, in what was undoubtedly the boldest stroke of the entire war Washington decided to attack two outposts at Bordentown and Trenton on the eastern bank of the Delaware River. In the event, Washington only had sufficient boats to transport his force across the Delaware River to carry out the attack against Trenton, which was held by the Hessians. This attack was to be carried out on Christmas Day when the Hessians would not have had a chance to recover from the previous night's celebrations.

The battle at Trenton and the subsequent battle of Princeton were probably Washington's finest tactical achievements during the American War of Independence. Success in these battles was essential to him, for it restored his reputation as a military leader with Congress and lifted the morale of the soldiers of the Continental Army, which had been so damaged by the recent reverses. Had he failed in these battles, it is likely that General Horatio Gates, who following his victory at Saratoga had become a public critic of Washington and contender for his post, would have succeeded him as commander-in-chief. If that had happened, then the American War of Independence might have ended very differently, for it is doubtful if Gates had the enduring qualities of leadership that could have turned so many initial American defeats into final victory.

Trenton lay across the Delaware River some 30 miles north of Philadelphia. It was garrisoned by 1,300 Hessian troops under command of Colonel Rahl, who had neglected to construct adequate defences of the town, including the digging of entrenchments – something that Howe had expressly ordered him to do. Nearly two years into the war, Washington had already established a good intelligence network throughout the colonies and was therefore well aware of the weakness of the German defences. Although he had surprise on his side, Washington was nevertheless conscious of the great risks that he was taking in launching a night-time attack. As he wrote to his friend Colonel Joseph Reed, 'Christmas day at night, one hour before day, is the time fixed upon for our attempt upon Trenton . . . our numbers, I am sorry to say, being less than I had any conception of. Yet nothing but dire necessity will, nay must, justify an attack.'

By last light, and in freezing weather, Washington concentrated his troops on the west bank of the Delaware River about 9 miles upstream of Trenton. He was accompanied by Greene, Sullivan and Lord Stirling. His trusted colonel Henry Knox was the beachmaster responsible for ferrying the troops across the river, the majority of them being transported in heavy Durham boats that were normally used to carry pig iron down the Delaware River. By 1800 hours, 2,400 troops with some cannon began crossing the icy river near McConkey's Ferry Inn. However, it was nearly four o'clock in the morning before all the artillery and troops were landed on the eastern bank and able to begin their approach march to Trenton. The attacking force was four hours behind schedule. Nevertheless, Washington felt that he was now committed and decided to push on. Forming into two columns, he led a left flanking attack, while Sullivan took his column along the lower river road directly to Trenton. It had begun to hail and snow as the Americans approached the Hessians, who were mostly asleep. At about eight o'clock, with everyone in place, Washington gave the order to Sullivan to fix bayonets and charge, for the muskets had become wet and useless during the crossing and approach march. The Hessian outposts were soon overwhelmed and Washington advanced with his artillery. The Hessians belatedly attempted a counterattack under Colonel Rahl, who was mortally wounded. By then the situation had become hopeless for the Hessians, who were surrounded on all sides. 'Sir, they have struck . . . their colours are down,' Captain Forest of the artillery shouted to his commander-in-chief. 'So they are!' replied Washington. The battle, which had lasted only an hour and a half, was over. The Americans had captured 1,000 Hessians along with their baggage and artillery with only a few losses. Amongst the victors was a future president of the United States, Lieutenant James Monroe, who was wounded in an attack against the Hessian artillery park. He carried a bullet in his shoulder for the remainder of his life. The Hessians had lost 114 men killed or wounded.

Unfortunately, the other two crossings over the Delaware River, one of which was destined to block an expected counterattack from strong Hessian positions to the south of Trenton, failed to take place. There was also a British infantry battalion stationed at Princeton half a day's march away, so Washington wisely decided to withdraw back across the Delaware River into Pennsylvania. But he did not altogether abandon his plans to drive the British from New Jersey. That night he dined with four captured Hessian officers at the Ferry Inn. One of them, a Lieutenant Piel, wrote, 'General Washington is a courteous and polite man, but very cautious and reserved, talks little and has a crafty physiognomy.'

The strategic importance of the battle was enormous. Having had such a clear demonstration of the dangers of leaving an open western flank from which his scattered forces could be attacked at will by the rebels, Howe became committed to a policy whose first priority was the destruction of Washington's army. This prevented him from making the planned move north up the Hudson River that was to take place later in the year. Such a move would have secured New England and thereafter allowed Howe to take on Washington in the south. This, after all, was the grand strategy that had been agreed with Lord Germain in London. The battle of Trenton set in train the events that were to lead to the catastrophic defeat of the British at Saratoga. As Germain put it, 'All our hopes are blasted by the unhappy affair.'

Surprised by the defeat at Trenton, Howe immediately ordered Cornwallis to block any further incursions into New Jersey by Washington, who on 29 December had already moved back across the Delaware River into a position just south of Trenton. At the same time, Howe landed a force of 1,000 men at Amboy north of Princeton.

Having heard that Cornwallis was heading south from Princeton on 2 January 1777 with an army 8,000 strong, Washington prepared strong defensive positions behind a small stream called Assunpink Creek. He also sent out Greene with orders to fire on the flanks of the approaching British columns. Thus, by the time Cornwallis reached the creek, the British forces had already been subjected to continuous harassing fire by Greene's troops during their approach march. Nevertheless, Cornwallis remained supremely confident of his ability to defeat Washington, even though by then the Americans were well entrenched.

Since it was late in the afternoon when he had come upon Washington's positions, Cornwallis decided to wait for reinforcements and attack the next day. 'At last we have run down the old fox, and we will bag him in the morning,' he wrote. This was not to be. The next morning, Cornwallis was awakened by the sound of cannon fire far to his rear in the direction of Princeton. Washington had simply slipped away in the night, leaving his campfires burning to confuse his enemy. For the first time he had refused a set-piece battle, preferring to engage in manoeuvre warfare.

By dawn, following an old Quaker road unguarded by the British, Washington had managed to bypass Cornwallis's forces and was now engaged with the British reinforcements that Cornwallis had demanded hurry to his support in Trenton. This reinforcing column was led by Colonel Mawhood. As he crossed a bridge some 2 miles south of Princeton, Mawhood had seen the flash of arms glinting in the early morning sun. Supposing them to be some remnant of a fleeing rebel group, he about-faced and attacked what was, in reality, a large detachment of Washington's force commanded by General Mercer. On seeing the approaching enemy, Mercer immediately formed his force into extended line and charged up a slope, arriving first on the high ground that separated the two opposing forces. The British responded to the rebels, opening shots by fixing bayonets and charging at the enemy, who were now on higher ground. This they succeeded in capturing, and in the ensuing fight Mercer was killed and the Americans fled in disorder pursued by the British.

However, Washington had heard the firing to his flank. He instantly ordered a detachment of Pennsylvania militia to advance to the support of Mercer. As the Americans emerged from a wood on his flank, Mawhood saw that any further pursuit would be foolhardy, as it would expose his men to defilade fire. He ordered his soldiers to halt and, forming up his artillery, opened fire on the rebel militia.

The Americans wavered. Washington had by then arrived on the scene and, seeing the attack falter, galloped forward under fire to rally his men. This bought sufficient time for the remainder of the American force to enter the battle.

Realizing that he was now outnumbered, Colonel Mawhood retreated with heavy loss towards Trenton. Meanwhile, the American advance guard under General Arthur St Clair had engaged another British regiment, also part of Mawhood's force, and sent them headlong in retreat back to Princeton, where they shortly after surrendered. Continuing the pursuit of the British towards the north, Washington finally halted near Kingston, halfway between Princeton and Brunswick, where the main British supply depot was based. Given that his men were exhausted, supplies were low and Cornwallis was already in pursuit to his rear, he wisely decided to head north-west to Morristown. Here Washington hoped that he would be able to spend the remainder of the winter unchallenged by the British. Morristown was located in heavily wooded, mountainous country and it was also the home of many rebels. It would be difficult for Cornwallis to surprise Washington there, and yet from this location Washington presented an ever present threat to the British. Howe was therefore compelled to withdraw his troops from the west part of New Jersey and await the spring before deciding what to do next.

The world was witnessing, in the words of Alexander Hamilton, 'the extraordinary spectacle of a powerful army straitened within narrow limits by the phantom of a military force'. One of the great advantages that Washington had over the British was the possession of better intelligence. This was to allow him to outmanoeuvre his enemy time and again throughout the remaining six years of war.

*

Soon after the outbreak of the American War of Independence, Congress appointed an agent in London telling him it was 'of utmost consequence to the cause of liberty that it be kept informed of developments in Europe'. Both sides in the conflict had set out to build effective intelligence networks but by the end of the war it was Washington who proved to have had a consistently better flow of intelligence. Using the insurgent militia as their ears and eyes, the Americans were able to develop wide-reaching sources of intelligence that allowed them early warning of most British moves. This was as true of the British invasions from Canada in 1776 and 1777 as it was of the operations of Cornwallis in the south during the last two years of the war.

Some of Washington's informants were genuine patriots, others were people who, as the war progressed, tried to ingratiate themselves with the winning side and, as in all conflicts, many others were prepared to pass information in return for payment. The existence of smugglers, privateers and a surprisingly large number of deserters from both sides meant that information could easily be passed across the battle lines. Although both sides tried hard to eliminate the spy rings operating against them – the usual fate of captured spies was execution – neither side was ever able to fully succeed in preventing a leak of intelligence to the other side.

In the early stages of the war, both sides focused on gaining tactical intelligence relating to the intentions, movements and strength of the enemy. Even before the British had landed on Long Island, Washington was warning his generals that 'Much will depend on early intelligence and meeting the enemy before they can entrench. I should much approve of small harassing parties . . . so they might keep the enemy alarmed and more than probably bring off a prisoner from whom some valuable intelligence may be obtained.'

However, as time went on, it became more important to discover the longer-term political goals and strategic objectives of the enemy, and Benjamin Franklin, who was Congress's ambassador in Paris, was able to collect much useful intelligence about future British intentions from not only his own numerous civilian contacts, but also the French government. The British, who also had well-placed sources in Paris, were less successful when it came to acquiring vital intelligence regarding the timely movement of the French fleet. In North America, Washington kept control of the entire rebel intelligence organization himself, including personally handing out money, giving instructions and briefing agents. Early on in his military career, in 1753, he had been sent on a highly successful intelligence-gathering mission against the French by Governor Robert Dinwiddie of Virginia and this experience was to prove extremely useful to him throughout the war.

However, his first attempt to infiltrate the British lines had not been as successful as his early missions against the French. In mid September 1776, he had despatched one of his young officers, Nathan Hale, a graduate of Yale, to Long Island to seek out information about the dispositions of the many British regiments garrisoned there. Hale set off disguised as a teacher, wearing a brown cloth suit and a broad-rimmed hat. Unfortunately for him his passage across Long Island Sound was observed by Robert Rogers, the commanding officer of the famous Rangers. He was finally tracked down to a roadside inn and, after incriminating himself in discussions with Rogers, was hanged on 22 September 1776. It had been a thoroughly amateur beginning.

After Howe had occupied New York, so the need to obtain timely and accurate information about the British plans grew more urgent for the rebels. For at that time

Howe had the ability to launch surprise attacks by sea almost anywhere along the American coastline, and also by land into New England from his bases in New York and New Jersey. After the successes of Trenton and Princeton, Washington had moved his headquarters and the remnants of his army to Morristown in New Jersey. It was here in the winter of 1776 that he set about building his first professional spy network. He had approached Congress to find a suitable person to head this nascent organization and a civilian named Nathaniel Sackett was duly chosen. But Washington also insisted that he should have a military deputy, since the principal requirement at that time was for tactical-level military intelligence. Washington appointed Benjamin Tallmadge to this post. He was a young officer in the Continental Light Dragoons who had been at Yale with Nathan Hale. Indeed, it had been Tallmadge who recruited Hale to be a spy.

Tallmadge proved to be an excellent choice, for after Sackett was dismissed for failing to provide Washington with the intelligence he required, he became Washington's spy chief and built one of the most successful spy rings that operated during the entire war – the Culper Ring. This ring was based in New York and provided Washington with vitally important pieces of intelligence including warning of the raids by Tryon into Connecticut and the arrival of Admiral Graves with naval reinforcements on 13 August 1780, which threatened the new French base in Rhode Island.

Meanwhile, the British were struggling to acquire the same quality of intelligence as the Americans. They never managed to develop a well-established network of spies and informers because they were unable to maintain a permanent presence in any part of North America – other than Georgia and New York – during the entire period of the war. Nevertheless, the British commander-in-chief, General Clinton, made every effort to develop an intelligence organization that was as effective as that of Washington. His efforts met with little success until a major breakthrough came for the British in May 1779 when they were able to recruit General Benedict Arnold to their side. Between that time and September 1780, when he was exposed by the capture of Major André, his go-between with Clinton, Arnold was able to furnish Clinton with such good top-level intelligence about rebel movements and intentions that Washington was, for a time, neutralized.

The key to winning insurgency wars or defeating terrorism is always intelligence. Without this, armies have to resort to harsh military measures that inevitably alienate the population. They have to employ the blunderbuss rather than the stiletto. Good intelligence on the other hand allows the security forces to operate selectively and lower their military profile. Furthermore, it is normally the continuous flow of low-level intelligence that is most useful to the security forces, for this allows them to penetrate the insurgent organization and ultimately control it. During the American War of Independence this was well understood by Washington, who saw that many small pieces of information could lead to valuable revelations.

The decision by Howe not to pursue Washington towards Morristown but withdraw his forces from most of New Jersey may have been tactically justifiable but it was disastrous from the point of view of winning the information battle. For this action demonstrated to the people of New Jersey, who had witnessed the opposing armies marching to and fro across their land, that they could no longer place any reliance on the British. So when George Washington, taking advantage of the absence of the British, called for the people of New Jersey to swear allegiance to the

United States, they did so in large numbers. Many had already been horrified by stories of rape, looting and violence committed by the Hessian troops – though there is some doubt as to whether these charges or indeed those directed elsewhere at British troops were justified. It is also true that the behaviour of the colonial militia had caused some concern to Washington regarding the ill-treatment of the civilian population. But by then the British were losing the all-important propaganda battle. The result was a dwindling of support for the British Crown amongst the hitherto uncommitted population in the thirteen colonies and a matching fall in the flow of intelligence to the British.

Today, in Iraq, it is the Americans who are losing the information battle because of the high levels of military force used and their close alliance with Israel. It has thus proven extremely difficult for the US to obtain intelligence about either the Iraqi insurgents or al-Qaeda terrorists. Since 2003, the Muslim world has been bombarded with horrific images of deaths, injuries and destruction caused by US military action in Iraq. These images have been shown by television stations such as Abu Dhabi TV and Al Jazeera, which Arabs and Muslims far prefer to watch rather than CNN or Fox TV. The fact that the insurgents in Iraq have themselves caused far more civilian casualties than the occupation forces counts for nothing in the war to win popular support. As in any counter-insurgency war, it is perceptions that count rather than realities. If a population becomes alienated from its government or national security forces, then a vital source of intelligence is shut off. Having lost the information battle, the flow of intelligence is thereafter always in favour of the insurgents.

As Washington said, 'the necessity of procuring good Intelligence is apparent & need not be further urged – All that remains for me to add is, that you keep the whole matter as secret as possible. For upon Secrecy, Success depends in Most Enterprises of the kind, and for want of it, they are generally defeated, however.' In this way, the man who was to become the first president of the United States summed up the critical military problem confronting his forty-second successor in Iraq. It is already evident that George Bush has been far less successful than George Washington when it comes to winning the information and intelligence battle. While the occupation forces in Iraq remain blinded by their lack of intelligence, the insurgents are able to live freely amongst the people and attack when the element of surprise is on their side. Given such an imbalance in the flow of intelligence, as the British discovered in North America in the eighteenth century, it is impossible to win an insurgency war.

Chapter Three

Never was there a finer example of the art of organising disaster.　　SIR JOHN FORTESCUE

By the start of 1777, the British grand strategy in North America was at the same deep level of confusion as the American strategy in Iraq had become after four years of struggle. The withdrawal of the British from Boston and New Jersey and the failure to establish a firm base in the south had given the initiative to the American rebels, at least for the time being. The hope that the American loyalists would rally in great numbers to the British cause had proved to be ill-founded. Washington remained undefeated in the west of New Jersey and Pennsylvania and as a result he retained a total freedom to manoeuvre and strike at the British at will. Furthermore, he was beginning to build up the regular component of his forces, having been promised by Congress a regular army eighty-eight battalions strong. By May, the army had reached a strength of more than 8,000 men, in spite of the smallpox that had swept through both the American and the British armies during the winter of 1777. (On the rebel side, Washington had introduced compulsory vaccination for his soldiers – something that was not done by the British.)

It became increasingly probable that the British would not easily crush the rebellion and the French would soon decide to enter the war on the side of the American insurgents. If this happened, then the British would be forced to maintain a higher level of naval presence in the Channel Approaches and this would prevent them from maintaining an effective blockade along the eastern seaboard of America. There was even a chance that the French might be able to gain naval superiority in North America. The overall balance of force was starting to turn against the British and decisive strategic action was clearly required. It was not to be forthcoming, because the political leaders in Britain and the generals on the ground in North America remained in a state of denial about the realities of the situation.

Howe remained convinced that the rebellion could still be finally crushed that summer. He believed that the majority of the people had tired of war and only desired peace and pardon. His spies informed him that there was a solid loyalist support in Pennsylvania on which he could count, though he estimated that he would still need an extra 20,000 troops to defeat Washington militarily – a figure that it was impossible for Britain to provide. In the event, only 5,500 troops were promised by Germain. Howe therefore withdrew 3,000 soldiers from Rhode Island in order to make up the necessary numbers for his forthcoming operation against the rebels in Pennsylvania. Although he left a small garrison in Newport to guard the British naval base, the result of this decision was to leave most of New England without a British presence and once more under the control of the rebels. It also left his rear unguarded and this, in the end, was to prove disastrous for the British. Howe and his masters in London were manifesting all the signs of those who have lost their strategic sense of direction, relying on what they want to believe rather than on what the harsh facts on the ground dictate. As General George Patton said more than two hundred years later: 'It is circumstances that should shape one's plan, not a plan the circumstances.'

By the spring of 1777 it should have been quite clear to British planners in both London and America that it was now impossible for the British to conduct a northern campaign aimed at seizing control of the Hudson Valley – thereby isolating New England – and at the same time mount operations against Washington's Continental Army. Without popular support, there were simply far too few British troops to accomplish both tasks simultaneously. Seduced by his own propaganda into believing that loyalist support in Pennsylvania and Maryland had stayed firm, when in fact it was fast evaporating, Howe made the strategically flawed decision to head south rather than go north to Albany to join forces with Burgoyne, who was about to invade America from Canada.

One of the indicators of a failing strategy is that it no longer reflects realities on the ground. Generals who develop an emotional attachment to their original strategy tend to respond to successive defeats by calling for more resources or dismissing setbacks as being tactically unimportant. Above all, they do not recognize that they have reached the culminating point in their campaign. This is the moment at which, no matter what they subsequently do, their existing strategy is bound to fail. The only proper course of action is to make radical changes to the strategic objectives. It may even be necessary to sue for peace and obtain whatever can be salvaged, for to continue is usually to lose everything.

The government at home will also usually have a major political stake in maintaining its original strategy, because its reputation depends on a successful outcome. It generally refuses, until too late, to admit that the original policies were wrong and take the painful decision to make the necessary changes. Meanwhile, civilians become wary of the lies and promises made to them by their political masters. This was the experience of the British during the war against the American rebels in 1777 when the British generals and their political leaders pushed relentlessly on, long after the strategic advantage had passed to the enemy.

The same phenomenon of denial could be seen emerging in the American and British administrations after four years of war in Iraq. The original objective of establishing an enduring democracy in Iraq and making that country an example for others to follow had clearly become impossible to achieve. Nevertheless, instead of recognizing the fact, they continued with the same policies and failing strategies. In a speech on 19 June 2006 President Bush still felt able to claim that in Iraq, 'we will inflict a major defeat on the terrorists, and we will show the world the power of a thriving demo-cracy in the heart of the Middle East'. He seemed entirely indifferent to the facts that the country was in chaos, the civilian death rate was running at 4,000 people a month and had now possibly reached a total of half a million deaths. Large segments of the Iraqi population, especially in Bagh-dad and Basra, had by mid 2006 transferred their loyalties to the militias in order to obtain some sort of security for themselves. They no longer believed in the American vision or that the current strategy can succeed. In this view they were supported by the majority of Americans.

The response of President Bush and also Prime Minister Blair to falling domestic support for the war in Iraq inevit-ably is to declare that defeat is not an option, as the withdrawal of American troops from Iraq would result in chaos as extremists and terrorists seize power in the Middle East. As in Vietnam, the domino theory had once again been resurrected to justify a continuation of present strategy. Yet when the Americans finally left Vietnam, the fear that

MICHAEL ROSE

Communism would spread throughout the Far East proved to be groundless. The fear that chaos will result in the Middle East following a US withdrawal from Iraq is, of course, equally groundless. George III similarly predicted that chaos would ensue following the British withdrawal from America which of course never happened.

Two and a quarter centuries before, Burgoyne was well aware of the dangers of attacking the rebels simultaneously on two fronts. He had made it quite plain to Germain while he had been in London that the operation to gain control of the Hudson River Valley would only succeed if Howe was ordered to move north from New York and join up with him at Albany. Burgoyne's expeditionary force would then have control of Lake Champlain and the upper Hudson Valley while Howe would take control of the valley from Albany to New York. The entire length of the Hudson Valley would have to be secured before there could be any movement south. In discussing the overall plan with Germain, he wrote, 'These ideas are formed upon the supposition that it be the sole purpose of the Canadian army to effect a junction with General Howe, or after co-operating so far as to get possession of Albany and open communication to New York, to remain upon the Hudson's River and thereby enable that general to act with his whole force to the southward.'

It was abundantly clear that the two different campaigns, the first to take control of the Hudson Valley and the second to seize Philadelphia, should have been sequential, not simultaneous. Germain even followed his discussions with Burgoyne by writing to Carleton, the British commander-in-chief in Canada, on 26 March 1777, instructing him in some detail as to how the northern invasion was to be mounted. The agreed plan envisaged Burgoyne with an army of 7,000 men advancing down Lake Champlain from the north towards Albany, while a smaller force of 700 men under Lieutenant Colonel Barry St Leger would approach Albany from the west along the line of the Mohawk River, thereby creating a diversion. Meanwhile, Howe was to move up the Hudson River from New York. It was to be a three-pronged attack. Carleton, in Canada, was instructed by Germain to send a copy of these instructions to Howe.

Although Germain knew of Howe's plan to concentrate his main effort in the south against Washington in Pennsylvania, instead of supporting Burgoyne in the Hudson Valley, he did not explicitly oppose the plan because he shared the same optimistic view about the weakness of the opposition and the strength of the loyalist support in the south. With the benefit of hindsight, the most generous assessment is that Germain thought that Howe would successfully complete his operation against Washington in sufficient time to move north to give Burgoyne the support that he expected. Whatever the truth, Germain undoubtedly failed to give the necessary orders directly to Howe that would have spelt out the phased nature of the plan and the degree of support that he was to give to Burgoyne.

Realizing that confusion was possible, one of Germain's secretaries, William Knox, pointed out that Howe had received no specific instructions regarding the agreed plan and offered to prepare a draft letter for Germain to sign. But Germain, who was about to set off for a weekend in the country, replied impatiently, 'So my poor horse must stand in the street all the time, and I shan't be to my time anywhere.' It was therefore decided that Germain would depart for his country home in Kent immediately and that a deputy undersecretary, Mr D'Oyly, would write to Howe enclosing copies of Germain's orders to Burgoyne. This was done, and in due course Howe acknowledged receipt of

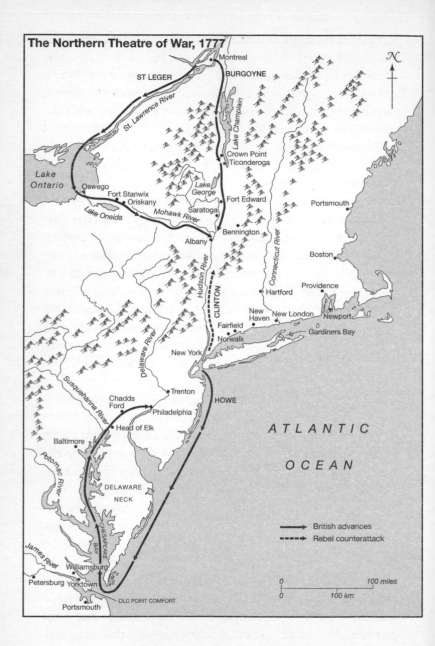

The Northern Theatre of War, 1777

N

ST LEGER

Montreal

BURGOYNE

St. Lawrence River

Lake Champlain

Crown Point
Ticonderoga

Lake
Ontario

Oswego

Fort Stanwix
Oriskany

Lake Oneida

Mohawk River

Lake
George

Fort Edward

Portsmouth

Saratoga

Bennington

Albany

Hudson River

Boston

Connecticut River

CLINTON

Hartford

Providence

New
Haven

New London

Newport

Delaware River

Fairfield

Norwalk

Gardiners Bay

New York

Susquehanna River

Trenton

HOWE

Chadds
Ford

Philadelphia

Head of Elk

Baltimore

ATLANTIC

OCEAN

Potomac River

DELAWARE

NECK

CHESAPEAKE BAY

James River

Williamsburg

Petersburg   Yorktown

OLD POINT COMFORT

Portsmouth

→ British advances

▶ Rebel counterattack

0   100 miles

0   100 km

both. But no copy of D'Oyly's letter was apparently ever made. Whatever it contained, it is clear that Howe was given too much latitude in the interpretation of his orders. In one of the most bizarre episodes of the entire British handling of the war, Howe had therefore been left with the impression that his main effort should still be concentrated in the south and that he only needed to detach a small force to assist Burgoyne. The blame for this fatal confusion must ultimately lie with Germain.

So, instead of concentrating their forces in the Hudson Valley where their most important strategic objective lay, the British were to disperse themselves from the Canadian border to Georgia across 1,000 miles of inhospitable country, much of it held by the rebels. This made it impossible for the already over-stretched British supply chain to cope simultaneously with the two separate tasks in the north and south. The British fleet was unable to reinforce the army in Canada, maintain the existing garrisons on the eastern seaboard of America and at the same time transport Howe's army from New York.

Delays in launching the two expeditionary forces inevitably ensued, and it was not until 25 August 1777 that Howe landed his army of 15,500 men at the Head of Elk, which lay at the northern tip of Chesapeake Bay. This was to be the starting point for his march on Philadelphia. It is extraordinary that he did not march the short distance from New York to Philadelphia, which would have taken no more than four days, rather than make a long sea passage. This was after all the route that Clinton was to follow in the reverse direction a few months later. En route, Howe had received Germain's letter of 26 March 1777 stating a fervent hope that Howe would take possession of Philadelphia in sufficient time to give Burgoyne the support that had been planned. If he had taken his army by land there is every possibility that he would have been able to accomplish his goal of capturing Philadelphia and still have had time to support Burgoyne. But, having already committed himself to an approach by sea – something that took two months to accomplish – there was no chance at all that this could be done. Fortuitously, Howe had heard of Burgoyne's successful capture of the key forts of Crown Point and Ticonderoga on Lake Champlain and was therefore able to reassure himself that his part in Burgoyne's campaign was no longer critical. He 'hoped that Burgoyne would not be prevented from pursuing the advantages he had gained'. It proved to be a forlorn hope.

Strategically, the American rebels did not regard Philadelphia as having either political importance or military significance. Indeed, Congress had already planned to evacuate the town and move some 50 miles to the west – first to Lancaster and then on to York. Washington had been kept well informed of Burgoyne's advance south but had remained ignorant of where Howe intended to land his forces, thinking at first that he would move up the Hudson River to meet Burgoyne. Thus, initially, he had prepared to march north to reinforce General Schuyler. After some weeks of marching and countermarching, 'compelled to wander about the country like the Arabs in search of corn', Washington finally heard the news that Howe had landed in Chesapeake Bay. 'Now, let all New England turn out and crush Burgoyne,' he wrote. Leaving General Schuyler to deal with Burgoyne in the north, he marched his army, now 16,000 strong, confidently south to do battle with Howe. It was by now a very different army from the one that he had led in the retreat from New York the previous year. John Adams this time commented favourably, 'the army . . . I find to be extremely well armed, pretty well clothed and tolerably disciplined'. Washington, ignoring the lessons of his defeat in New York, believed that his newly re-formed army could defeat the British in a single decisive battle. He therefore decided to abandon his Fabian strategy and take on Howe before he could reach Philadelphia: 'Two years we have maintained the war and struggled with difficulties innumerable, but the prospect has brightened. Now is the time to reap the fruit of all our toils and dangers. If we behave like men this third campaign will be our last.'

Keeping a careful watch on the British as they disembarked at Head of Elk, Washington decided to defend the high ground at a place called Chadds Ford where the road between Baltimore and Philadelphia crossed Brandywine Creek. He arrived with his army at Chadds Ford on 9 September 1777 and prepared strong defensive positions on the eastern side of the river, at the same time pushing out patrols on the opposite bank to warn of Howe's approach. The following day, Howe concentrated his forces at a place called Kennett Square about 4 miles to the west. His objective was Philadelphia, which was 30 miles away. Using the same battle-winning tactics that he had employed on Long Island, Howe despatched Lord Cornwallis on a flanking move 12 miles to the west, where he was able to cross a fork of Brandywine Creek unopposed by the American rebels.

At ten o'clock in the morning on 11 September 1777, 5,000 Hessian and British troops under General Knyphausen, supported by artillery, launched a fierce attack on the centre of Washington's position across Brandywine Creek at Chadds Ford. Meanwhile, on the right of Washington's main defensive position, Cornwallis had moved fast and by midday was starting to engage rebel patrols to the right and rear of the Americans. It had been a foggy morning and Washington remained uncertain about the direction from which the main British attack was coming. At about two o'clock in the afternoon, a local man called Thomas Cheyney galloped up to Washington and excitedly told him that British troops were now behind them.

Washington did not believe this piece of information as he had already sent out a reconnaissance party under a Colonel Bland to give early warning of any threat from the right flank and no such movement by the British had been reported. However, less than an hour later the reconnaissance party reported back, confirming that a large British contingent under Cornwallis was already behind them and about to cut off the American line of retreat. Washington immediately ordered a counterattack on the centre against Knyphausen, presumably hoping to break through the British centre and so threaten Cornwallis with envelopment. This attack was soon driven back. Fortunately for the rebels, Washington had at the same time detached his right wing under Sullivan to block Cornwallis. He had also called up reinforcements under Greene to fill the gap that had been left by Sullivan on the right. Sullivan therefore took up a hastily prepared position around a large building called the Birmingham Meeting House on the Chester road, along which Cornwallis was now fast approaching. Meanwhile, Washington, anxious about the threat from Cornwallis, had decided to see how things were developing on his right flank. Guided by an elderly local farmer called Joseph Brown, he set off in the direction of the meeting house at a fast gallop, shouting somewhat ungraciously to Brown, 'Push along old man, push along old man.'

At four o'clock in the afternoon, the Cornwallis advance guard appeared in front of Sullivan's hastily prepared defensive position. In fierce fighting around the Birmingham Meeting House, Sullivan managed to hold up Cornwallis's advance for sufficient time to allow the main American force in the centre, which was still being pressed by the British, to make good its escape towards Chester. Meanwhile, Greene had covered 4 miles in forty-five minutes to take up a defensive line about a mile to the rear of what had been the main American position, and in a sharp engagement held off an attack by the British vanguard as the rebels withdrew. This action allowed Sullivan and the main rebel force to get away under cover of darkness, without the withdrawal becoming a rout. Washington had once again been outgeneralled by Howe, but he had nevertheless managed to make good his escape. The Americans lost 1,000 men and eleven pieces of artillery, while the British lost approximately half that number. Had Howe not deliberately left one of his cavalry regiments behind in New York, there is a good chance that he could have followed up the retreating Americans and inflicted even greater damage.

However, the rebel army suffered further losses a week later when a group of Pennsylvania militia under command of General Anthony Wayne was surprised at a place called Paoli's tavern by a British unit commanded by General Grey. It had succeeded in creeping up on the Americans partly because Grey had ordered that only bayonets were to be used by his troops and partly because the rebel sentries were asleep. In the ensuing slaughter, the British put to death and wounded 460 Americans. This became known as the Paoli massacre and set the scene for many subsequent atrocities between the two opposing forces. Thereafter Grey was always known as 'No Flints Grey'.

Two weeks later, on 26 September 1777, British forces marched into Philadelphia unopposed and stabled their horses in the town hall where the Declaration of Independence had been signed fifteen months previously. It had been an ignominious end to Washington's plan to decisively defeat the British. However, while the American Army may have been beaten, this setback in no way diminished the revolutionary spirit of the rebels. 'Come on boys, we shall do better another time,' was the cry and Congress voted thirty hogsheads of rum to the army. The American War of Independence still had six years to run.

In the eighteenth century, the American revolutionaries evidently understood that the loss of a capital city, or the changing of a regime, did not mean the end of the insurgency, for the vital ground in such wars is the attitude of the people. Amherst had already refused to accept command of the British Army in North America, presumably on the grounds that, as Wellington later said, the Americans had 'neither a head nor heart to cut off'. Thus, even though they had lost their capital city, by 1777 the American revolutionaries had not been eliminated and were still well supported by a growing number of the population of the thirteen colonies. In Iraq, the American commander-in-chief, President George Bush, clearly did not understand this basic rule of insurgency warfare. For although the armed forces of Saddam Hussein were decisively defeated in conventional terms in the spring of 2003, 'the remnants' were to form the kernel of the insurgency that it has ultimately proved impossible for the Americans to crush. Conventional military forces can never defeat a national movement of resistance, as the American Revolutionary War so well demonstrates.

Believing that his mission had been accomplished and Washington could offer no further significant threat, Howe split his forces. He established his main force of 8,000 troops at Germantown 5 miles north-west of Philadelphia and a garrison force within the city of 3,000 troops. The remainder of his troops were sent back to New Jersey. Meanwhile, his officers settled down to a social life filled with dinner parties, balls and theatre-going. On hearing that he had dispersed his forces, Washington, whose troops now outnumbered those of Howe, determined to mount what was in effect a revenge attack against the British at Germantown for what had happened at Paoli and Brandywine.

Germantown was at that time no more than a crossroads in the middle of a long piece of eighteenth-century ribbon development that straggled on either side of the road leading north-west out of Philadelphia. Twelve miles down that road was Washington's camp at Skippack Creek. Just beyond the Germantown crossroads was a large stone house that was the home of the Pennsylvania chief justice, Benjamin Chew. It was now occupied by a Colonel Musgrove of the British 40th Regiment, who was using it as his headquarters.

Washington attacked Germantown at dawn on 4 October 1777 when a dense fog covered his approach march. His plan was a complicated four-pronged attack involving one column under Greene attacking the right wing of the British Army, a second column under his command advancing down the main Philadelphia road and launching a simultaneous attack on the British centre, while the rebel militia were directed to attack the extreme left and right flanks of the British defensive position.

However, the same poor visibility that had made command and control so difficult at Brandywine had a similarly disastrous impact on the rebels at Germantown. The first exchange of fire was between Washington's advance guard and a piquet of the British light infantry, who after several gallant charges were unable to halt the progress of the Americans. The British fell back, leaving their commander Colonel Musgrove isolated in Chew's house. On seeing that he was surrounded, Colonel Musgrove slammed the heavy front door of the building shut and along with twenty men positioned himself behind the heavily shuttered windows, firing at the passing American soldiers. This action caused the rebels a fatal interruption to their advance and as a result all contact was lost between the centre and flanking formations. The smoke from the artillery and musket fire on both sides had reduced visibility even further to 30 yards. What had been a carefully coordinated plan of attack by Washington turned into a series of small, isolated engagements. Greene had meanwhile made good progress in the north, but his sudden appearance on the left flank of General Wayne, who was leading the American advance, caused panic in the ranks of the American soldiers, who thought that he was the enemy. They fell back and in spite of the efforts of their officers to rally them, what might have been a turning point in the battle in the American favour quickly turned into a rout.

Defeat had occurred as a result of a combination of events that neither Washington nor his officers had been able to control. It was the battle of Germantown that finally compelled Washington to accept the unpalatable fact that his newly formed Continental Army could not yet engage on equal terms with the British regulars. The British officers had, after all, succeeded in maintaining good control of their formations in the same difficult circumstances as those that faced the Americans. It was to be another four and a half years before Washington felt able to order a general action against the British and by then his army had, of course, been critically reinforced by seasoned French troops. The decision to adopt an insurgency approach to the war was finally taken by Washington after the battle of Germantown, in spite of the fact that the war in the north was going in favour of the Americans.

For while Washington had been unsuccessfully engaged in attacking the main British force in Pennsylvania, the

Continental Army in the north, commanded by General Horatio Gates, had successfully defeated and captured the entire British expeditionary force commanded by General Burgoyne at Saratoga.

General Carleton, the commander-in-chief in Canada, had been passed over by Germain for command of the expeditionary force that was to head into the Hudson Valley and his troops had been given to Burgoyne, who was his junior in rank. When he tried to resign the King refused to accept his resignation and he was forced to soldier on. He successfully disguised his true feelings when dealing with Burgoyne, but it was not surprising that there was some lack of support from Carleton with regard to the British plan.

In spite of being short of troops and logistic supplies, Burgoyne finally left Canada in June 1777 with high hopes of success against the rebels. Since his arrival in Canada on 6 May 1777 his time had been taken up with assembling and preparing his army for the difficult task ahead. Burgoyne understood that he would need a sizeable army to march on Albany from Canada, but the British government had repeatedly refused to provide the numbers of troops that he needed, choosing instead to reinforce Howe in the south. Burgoyne's plan had also depended on 2,000 loyalist troops and at least 1,000 irregular Indians being made available to him in Canada, but less than half that number had volunteered. The size of the army at the start of his expedition was therefore 7,863 men – less than half the number that he had hoped for. However, his officers were good, his soldiers well trained and they were well supported by artillery.

Unfortunately, through no fault of Burgoyne's, the entire world had become aware that an army was being prepared to march south from Canada in order to gain control of the

Hudson River. After all, a similar attempt had been made a year earlier under Carleton. Thus, the element of surprise that had been maintained by the rebel force under Arnold when he had marched north into Canada through the forests of New England in 1775 was to be denied to the British. Every step that Burgoyne took was known to Washington, his generals and, importantly, also the rebellious people of New England through whose countryside Burgoyne was soon to pass.

The settlers of New England were now generally so hostile to the British that they would rather burn their houses and crops than allow them to be taken by Burgoyne's troops. They were also prepared to join the militia to fight to keep the British from occupying their lands. It was therefore necessary for Burgoyne to secure a lengthy logistic supply chain that led back to Canada. Although it was possible to use the St Lawrence River and Lake Champlain for the first part of the journey, subsequently all his military supplies had to be dragged by teams of horses through the forests and swamps that separated Lake Champlain from the Hudson River. Most difficult to move were the larger artillery pieces and ammunition that he planned to take south from Ticonderoga. Burgoyne's plan also required a stockpile of thirty days' combat supplies to be built up when his force reached Fort Edward on the Hudson River before any attack was to be launched on Albany.

The problems posed by this long logistic chain were compounded by Burgoyne's decision in September 1777 to move overland from Skenesborough to Fort Edward along a forest track. He had made fast progress from Canada and had taken the forts of Crown Point and Ticonderoga almost without a shot being fired. On 7 July 1777, his forces under Brigadier General Fraser had overrun a rebel delaying position at Hubbardton, south of Ticonderoga, and they had inflicted considerable casualties on the rebels. By 11 July 1777, Burgoyne had established himself at Skenesborough at the southern end of Lake Champlain and he was preparing to move further south with the aim of capturing Fort Edward on the upper reaches of the Hudson River. The distance to Fort Edward was 23 miles if travelled via the difficult forest route directly south from Skenesborough.

Burgoyne had rejected the idea of following a shorter 16-mile route, which offered better going from the southern end of Lake George to Fort Edward, because this would mean 'a retrograde motion' back to Ticonderoga – Burgoyne did not like the idea of giving up ground that he had already taken from the retreating rebels. The Lake George route would also require a difficult 300-foot-high portage for the ferry boats from Ticonderoga to Lake George. Burgoyne therefore decided to continue the advance directly from Skenesborough, taking with him only light artillery and equipment. His heavy guns and equipment were to follow on later using the Lake George route. With hindsight it is clear that Burgoyne's ignorance of the difficulty of the terrain, choice of route and the effect of distance made his plan logistically unsustainable.

By the time it reached Fort Edward, Burgoyne's army was exhausted by its rapid progress and it had also outrun its supplies. As the British advanced their lines of communication became increasingly stretched, while those of the rebels were getting shorter. Meanwhile, the weather was deteriorating, with heavy rain making movement extremely difficult. Burgoyne's difficulties were further compounded by the delaying tactics of the retreating rebels, who had felled trees across the narrow track and destroyed all bridges as they went. As a result of these cumulative difficulties, a critical delay occurred in what should have been a fast-moving offensive and it was therefore not until 30 July 1777 that Burgoyne reached Fort Edward on the Hudson River. This delay gave the Americans the extra time that they vitally needed in order to prepare a main defensive position on the Hudson River north of Saratoga and reinforce their retreating army with militia.

If Burgoyne had been able to move sufficiently fast early in the summer of 1777, he would certainly have been able to reach Albany, for at that time the rebel army was both weak and disorganized. Command of the northern rebel army was being continually switched between Schuyler and Gates, depending on who had the ear of Congress at any particular moment. The rebel army was small in number and lacked supplies. In particular, the defences of Ticonderoga were so run down that the commander of the fort, General St Clair, announced late in June that he saw 'not the least prospect of our being able to defend the post unless the militia come in'.

Burgoyne's original plan had consisted of two diversionary attacks, one launched from Lake Ontario along the line of the Mohawk River and one deep into Connecticut to the east. Both of them, it was hoped, would draw off American forces from his main line of advance. The planned attack into Connecticut had not been agreed by Germain in London, but Burgoyne continued with his plan to attack from Lake Ontario in spite of the fact that this would take troops away from his under-strength force. This diversionary attack was to be commanded by Lieutenant Colonel Barry St Leger.

St Leger's first task was to seize Fort Stanwix, which lay at the head of the Mohawk River and which was strongly held by the rebels. On 6 August 1777, while laying siege to this fort, St Leger heard that a large rebel relief force of about 800 men was approaching from the south-east along the line of the Mohawk River under Nicholas Herkimer, a colonel of the local Tryon county militia. Accordingly, St Leger despatched a force of 900 Iroquois Indians supported by 450 men, comprising Sir John Johnson's King's Royal Regiment of New York, to intercept this ad hoc rebel army.

Relying on local Indian knowledge of the area, particularly that of the Mohawk war leader Joseph Brant, and repeating the same tactics used to defeat Braddock, the Iroquois decided to establish an ambush position in a small ravine about 6 miles east of Fort Stanwix. The ambush took the form of a horseshoe, with the British troops providing the blocking force and the Indians on the flanks. Herkimer's men walked straight into the trap. Ironically, Herkimer had earlier halted and refused to move any further forward because of the possibility of ambush in such broken country. He had wanted to send forward a reconnaissance party before moving his main force across the ravine, but on being accused of cowardice by his officers, he had ignored his best instincts and pressed forward.

As the militia, with Herkimer leading the way, were crossing the Oriskany Creek, which runs through a deep ravine, the ambush was sprung. Herkimer was immediately wounded but continued to issue orders while propped up against a tree and still smoking his pipe. A sortie was mounted from Fort Stanwix to help relieve the pressure on Herkimer's troops. This gallant action, coupled with a violent thunderstorm that interrupted the battle, allowed Herkimer finally to reorganize his hard-pressed formations and begin an orderly withdrawal. His men carried him from the battlefield but he later died of his wounds. Although the battle did not last long, it proved to be the fiercest battle of the entire Revolutionary War in terms of the proportion of casualties lost by both sides: the Tryon militia casualties amounted to 670 men killed or wounded out of 800, while the British lost some 150. Nevertheless, although the battle was considered a tactical defeat for the Americans, it prevented St Leger from advancing further down the Mohawk River valley or making a rendezvous with Burgoyne. He was forced to remain at Fort Stanwix where he continued the siege.

With Burgoyne having now reached Fort Edward, only two days' march from Albany, and with his army still in dire need of reinforcements, it was vitally important to the rebel General Schuyler that St Leger's force be finally dealt with, as it still posed a serious threat from the west. He therefore sent his best general, Benedict Arnold, to attack the British at Fort Stanwix. On hearing that the main component of the British force consisted of Iroquois Indians, Arnold employed one of the greatest acts of deception of the entire war. He sent a halfwit, who not only knew the Indians but also spoke their language fluently, to tell them that a large force of rebels numbering thousands of troops under command of Benedict Arnold was approaching Fort Stanwix. When asked by the Indians how many people were in this force, the man is reputed to have looked up and replied, 'as many leaves as there are in this forest'. Arnold's force actually consisted of less than a thousand men. Nevertheless, on hearing this news the Indians fled and St Leger was forced to give up the siege and retreat back into Canada. The local people still claim that Fort Stanwix was the first place in which a stars and stripes flag was flown in the face of the enemy and the only fort never to be taken in war.

The strategic lesson that can be drawn from the failure of St Leger's diversionary expedition was that the British plan relied too heavily on Indians whose loyalty, like that of any irregular force, would always lie with the winning side. It also seriously underestimated the support for the revolution amongst the colonists of New England. For Herkimer had been able to raise a force of 850 irregular soldiers in only a few hours from the population in the Mohawk Valley, which at that time consisted mainly of Dutch and German settlers. These men had stood and fought and died for a cause that was quite distant to them, probably because they so greatly disliked both the English and the Indians. In insurgency wars, the mass of the population generally first tries to avoid becoming involved in the war, but as soon as they or their families are directly threatened they resort to arms and side with whoever they think will give them most security. As the war progressed, and as they saw the destruction wrought by the British, more people became prepared to accept the alternatives of 'liberty or death'.

Another demonstration of the American insurgents' ability to rally people quickly to their cause came soon after the battle at Oriskany on 16 August 1777 when Burgoyne agreed to send a detachment of Germans to raid a rebel supply depot at Bennington. This was some 30 miles to the east of their location in the Hudson River Valley and well off their line of march. However, Burgoyne's army was running short of supplies and the temptation to divert a sizeable component of his force to obtain supplies was irresistible – especially when a move to the east also threatened the rebel heartlands of New England. The detachment was led by Lieutenant Colonel Friedrich Baum and consisted of 700 regular Hessian dragoons and 700 local loyalists, Canadians and Indians.

However, in mid July, fearing that Burgoyne might head east, the rebels had assembled a force of 1,500 New Hampshire and Massachusetts militiamen to defend their frontier. This force was led by John Stark, a woodsman who had fought in the French and Indian War with Rogers' Rangers. Stark had distinguished himself in the battle of Bunker Hill but, having been passed over by Congress for promotion, he had refused to place himself under orders of the Continental Army, preferring to remain under the orders of the General Court, the legislature of New Hampshire. Within a couple of weeks, twenty-five companies of men signed up – more than 10 per cent of the eligible males in the state.

On 13 August 1777, contact was made between the two forces on the Walloomsac River about 4 miles west of Bennington. Baum's orders were that if he was confronted by a strong rebel force he was to dig in and send for help. Accordingly, he deployed his force on the high ground on the north side of the river and waited for the arrival of the reinforcements. It was pouring with rain and this prevented any chance of immediate attack by the rebels. Four miles to the east, Stark also decided to wait, in his case until the weather had cleared. Realizing that the Hessians were thinly spread, his plan was to encircle the German positions and attack simultaneously from the front and flanks. He was reported to have declared before launching this attack, 'There are the redcoats and they are ours, or Molly Stark sleeps a widow tonight.'

On the afternoon of 16 August 1777, the weather cleared and Stark ordered his men to attack. He had already heard that Hessian reinforcements under Colonel Breymann were approaching from the west. The battle lasted two hours. Having first overrun the loyalist and Indian positions on the flanks, the rebels were able to turn their full attention to the Hessians in the centre, whom they now outnumbered. In spite of fierce German defensive fire from cannon and musket, the Americans succeeded in gaining entry to the main Hessian redoubt. Using their bayonets and muskets as clubs, they drove the dragoons from their position into the surrounding countryside where they were killed. Baum was mortally wounded, and the Germans surrendered.

As this battle ended, Breymann arrived with the Hessian reinforcements. It was too late to save Baum, but seeing that the Americans were in some disarray – both looting and attending to their wounded – the Germans mounted an immediate counterattack. But after hastily forming a skirmishing line, Stark was able to hold the Hessians until a group of several hundred Vermont militiamen commanded by Seth Warner arrived on the scene. These were the remnants of the force that had been defeated by the British at Hubbardton a month before and they were keen to take revenge. Using a combination of cannon and bayonet after fierce fighting they were able finally to rout Breymann's force.

The German losses at Bennington were 200 dead and 700 captured, while the American losses amounted to no more than 40 dead and 30 wounded. It had been a great American victory and one that showed that a rebel militia force could defeat even the most disciplined European soldiers.

Meanwhile, Burgoyne's offensive spirit was about to face its greatest test at the battle of Saratoga. This is traditionally known as the turning point of America's Revolutionary War. In fact, the battle of Saratoga consisted of two quite separate engagements. The first, somewhat indecisive engagement took place at Freeman's Farm on 19 September 1777, and the second on Bemis Heights nearly three weeks later on 7 October 1777. It was this latter battle that ended with the surrender of Burgoyne's army and marked the beginning of the end of British rule in America. For within a month of this defeat, the French government that had been wavering in its support for the American rebellion, sent £1m to Congress and within a year France had despatched a large expeditionary force across the North Atlantic.

On 13 September, Burgoyne had begun once again his slow advance south towards Albany. Breaking all contact with Canada, he evacuated the defensive positions to his rear, including Fort Edward, so that there could be no turning back. The entire British grand strategy was now dependent on success in the forthcoming battle. But he revealed his considerable misgivings in a letter to Germain when he wrote that he hoped 'circumstances will be such that my endeavours may be in some degree assisted by a co-operation of the army under Sir William Howe'. By then he knew that there was actually no hope of significant reinforcement from the south, and this letter represented a clear attempt to spread the blame for what he could already see might be a terrible British disaster, for the rebel resist-ance was becoming significantly greater as he headed south. As a rebel officer put it, 'his Army is drove to desperation and a most bloody Battle must ensue'.

His forces now numbered around 7,000 regular British and German troops who were supported by 1,000 militia, loyalists, Canadians and Indians. Surprisingly, Burgoyne was still accompanied by the 300 navy sailors who had been used to build bridges for the transport of his artillery during the long march south. Nevertheless, since leaving Canada, Burgoyne had lost more than a quarter of his strength and his troops were becoming exhausted. More importantly, he had lost the support of the Indians on whom he entirely depended for intelligence about the whereabouts of the enemy.

Six weeks earlier, a young girl called Jane McCrae had been murdered and scalped by Burgoyne's Indians. Burgoyne had been horrified by the incident, as had all Americans. In order to prevent any further damage to the reputation of his army, he had demanded that those responsible should be executed. Although this was never done, Burgoyne had additionally ordered that no Indian war parties should be deployed without a British commander. This caused a great number of defections amongst the Indians, for whom looting and scalping were the only reasons for fighting. By the beginning of September most of Burgoyne's Indian auxiliaries had left and this significantly reduced the reconnaissance capability of the British. Henceforth Burgoyne would be like a blind man striking out in the dark. This loss of Indian support was to prove a decisive element in his defeat at Saratoga.

The US made a similar mistake shortly after the fall of Saddam Hussein in 2003 when the de-Ba'athification programme denied the Coalition forces the services of the only people who could at that time have provided them with effective intelligence. They were people who had formerly worked in Saddam Hussein's intelligence apparatus and security forces, and many would have been prepared to switch their allegiance to the Americans. Indeed, some tried to do so but were turned away. Inevitably, as time went on, even those who might have supported the occupation forces started to react against the heavy-handed tactics employed by the American soldiers, not only in places like Abu Ghraib but more widely during routine search missions in pursuit of the remnants of Saddam Hussein's political and military apparatus. They saw US soldiers killing unarmed civilians without apparent accountability, although in some instances blood money was paid by the Coalition Provisional Authority. But it was the universal public humiliation of individual Iraqis who were paraded hooded and handcuffed on television or ill-treated in front of their families that was particularly offensive to Iraqis, for they are a people who value pride and honour before life itself.

Even the United Nations special representative in Baghdad, Sérgio Vieira de Mello, who was so tragically killed in the bombing of the UN headquarters in August 2003, vigorously protested at the time about the heavy-handed treatment of the Iraqis by American troops, but this did nothing to lessen the harshness of the tactics employed. His long experience of peacekeeping and nation-building enabled him to see how damaging in the long term this ill-treatment of the Iraqis was to the American cause. He was ignored, and the key people who could have provided the Americans with vital intelligence against the insurgents finally took sides against them and joined the insurgency along with large sections of the Iraqi population.

In September 1777, in great contrast to their successors in Iraq, the rebel military commanders in New England had an endless flow of excellent intelligence concerning Burgoyne's movements not only from the local population, but from their scouts as well. Furthermore, as a result of an increasing number of desertions from the British Army, the Americans were also aware of the fast-deteriorating conditions the British soldiers were facing who were, by then, having to survive on half-rations. As news of the faltering British advance spread, so large numbers of militia soldiers flocked to join Gates's army. Many had been appalled by not only the scalping of Jane McCrae, but also the general behaviour of the British troops, as well as the Germans, who had been burning houses and taking corn and livestock. The settlers were determined to protect their homes at all costs. As a result Gates succeeded in building up his troop numbers to a level where they constituted twice the British strength. All these factors kept the morale of the rebels exceptionally high.

Gates was well liked by his soldiers and although he was cautious to a degree, he was a professional soldier who understood conventional warfare. He had realized that by September the balance of forces had turned firmly in his favour. For the first time in months, the Americans had stopped retreating and were now advancing north towards the British. Their army was now almost 15,000 strong and it contained the most experienced of all rebel commanders, Benedict Arnold. It also included Daniel Morgan, whose corps of Pennsylvania riflemen was reckoned by Washington to be the 'finest infantry of the day'. Both were to prove critical to the defeat of the British in the days to come.

About 9 miles south of Saratoga, the British crossed over to the west bank of the Hudson River. Here the rebels had occupied a location known as Bemis Heights. This was a thickly wooded plateau that dominated the route along the west bank of the Hudson River – a position that Burgoyne would be forced to take. It had been strongly fortified by a Polish military engineer named Thaddeus Kosciusko, who had immigrated to America in 1776 and subsequently volunteered to serve in the Continental Army in the rank of colonel. He had been educated at the Royal Military School in Warsaw and the School of Artillery and Engineering in France and was one of the foreign military officers who brought a much-needed technical expertise into Washington's newly formed army.

Burgoyne knew that he could not attack the strong American position head on, especially as the intervening country was broken by deep ravines. Neither was he able to force a passage between the high ground and the river because the route was well defended and covered by rebel artillery. He therefore chose to attempt to outflank the rebels by seizing an unoccupied hill to the west of their main position. It was on this hill that Freeman's Farm was located, in the middle of a clearing. From there, hoping to repeat his successful capture of Ticonderoga, he would be able to threaten Bemis Heights with artillery fire. However, because of the lack of intelligence he had no idea of the whereabouts of the enemy patrols and picquets that had undoubtedly been sent out by Gates. He therefore decided to attack on all fronts.

If Burgoyne had been aware of the American dispositions on Bemis Heights, he could have feinted in the centre and left, and placed the major effort of his attack on his right flank. Had he done this, he would have almost certainly been able to capture the high ground to the north of the American defensive position, onto which he could then have directed observed artillery fire. This was his only hope of success, for he was too weak in numbers ever to mount a direct attack against such a strong position.

But without the necessary intelligence Burgoyne was forced to divide his forces into three columns. Major General Riedesel was given command of the left column of German troops and had orders to move along the river road before swinging west to join the main force. Brigadier General James Hamilton, accompanied by Burgoyne, commanded the centre with four British battalions. Brigadier General Simon Fraser led the right wing with both the light infantry and grenadier battalions. His orders were to turn the American left flank.

On 19 September – the day of the battle of Freeman's Farm – the British got off to a bad start. An early morning fog delayed the launching of the attack, and it was nearly ten o'clock before it had sufficiently burned off and Burgoyne's forces were able to get under way. As communication was so difficult in the wooded terrain, Burgoyne decided to ride with Hamilton. Since he would be out of touch with his left flank, he told Riedesel that the signal for him to switch his line of approach away from the river to the centre would be three cannon shots. This would be given if Hamilton came under extreme pressure from the rebels. Meanwhile, Fraser on the right was an experienced

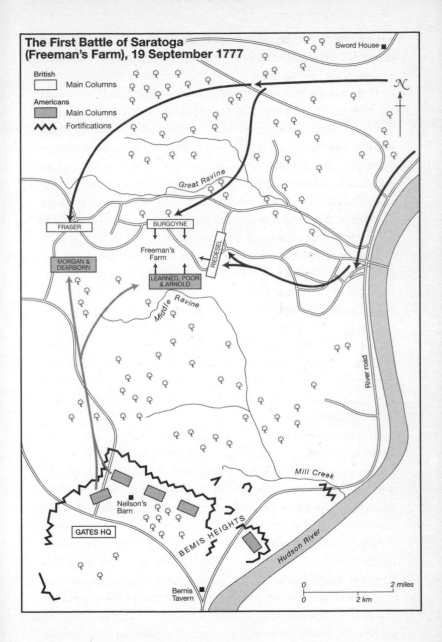

The First Battle of Saratoga (Freeman's Farm), 19 September 1777

British
Main Columns

Americans
Main Columns

Fortifications

Sword House

N

Great Ravine

FRASER

BURGOYNE

Freeman's Farm

MORGAN & DEARBORN

LEARNED, POOR & ARNOLD

RIEDESEL

Middle Ravine

Neilson's Barn

GATES HQ

Mill Creek

BEMIS HEIGHTS

River road

Hudson River

Bemis Tavern

0   2 miles
0   2 km

commander whom Burgoyne could rely on to read the battle for himself.

In the American camp there was disagreement about how to respond to the forthcoming British attack. Gates had decided on a defensive strategy which consisted of engaging the British from behind the protection of his strongly fortified position. However, Arnold believed that fighting such fixed battles gave the advantage to the British and he persuaded a reluctant Gates to allow him to make a preliminary strike at the approaching British. Taking Morgan's rifles, Dearborn's infantry and two New Hampshire militia brigades under command of Ebenezer Learned and Enoch Poor, he set off to locate the British.

Meanwhile, the British had found the going to be more difficult than they had anticipated. It took them four hours before Hamilton's vanguard, under command of an experienced British officer, Major Forbes, had arrived at Freeman's Farm, roughly midway between the two camps. As Forbes's soldiers emerged into the clearing around the farmhouse, it immediately came under fire from what Forbes thought was a rebel outpost. In fact, it was the advance party of the main rebel force under Daniel Morgan, who had already arrived at the farm. Invisible to the British, and firing from the surrounding woods, the Americans took a heavy toll of the redcoats and forced Forbes to retreat back into cover with considerable loss of men. Morgan's riflemen gave chase across the clearing but were nearly annihilated by Fraser, who had rushed to the sound of the gunfire and had surprised them on their open left flank. By then Hamilton had arrived on the scene and was forming his troops into line for a second attack.

On his right, Fraser did not pursue Morgan very far, and Morgan was soon able to re-form his men and continue to attack the hard-pressed British centre, this time from a position that was out of Fraser's view. Because Fraser had stuck so narrowly to his orders to secure the high ground on the right of the British advance, he failed to press home his initial surprise attack on the exposed left flank of the rebels, and Hamilton's small force of 2,000 men was left on its own to receive the entire weight of the American onslaught. Lack of manoeuvrability had once again proved to be a serious weakness of British tactics.

By sending his forces along three separate approach routes that were so far apart in what was, and still is, extremely difficult broken country, Burgoyne was unable to deploy his reserve forces to where the main American resistance finally developed. By the time that Riedesel arrived to reinforce the beleaguered British centre, the rebels had already inflicted a significant level of casualties on the British side. Thus, when the rebels finally realized that they were outnumbered and decided to retreat, it was too late for the British to pursue them. Tactical momentum had been lost and the British were not subsequently able to recover it.

At an earlier point in the battle, Gates – who is reputed never to have left his rear headquarters near Neilson's Barn, which was out of sight to the rear – had ordered up two New Hampshire regiments to support Morgan. For the next three hours the battle raged to and fro across the clearing around Freeman's Farm, with the British artillery pieces changing hands several times. It was only with the arrival of the German troops under Riedesel, four hours after the start of the main battle, that the fight finally went in favour of the British. It was then that the Americans decided to retreat back to their main fortified position on Bemis Heights, which had not yet been subjected to any attack by the British.

Although the British may have been left masters of the

field, their losses had amounted to 600 men. A young British officer, Lieutenant Anburey, commented after the battle, 'I am fearful the real advantages resulting from this hard-fought battle will rest on that of the Americans . . .' The Americans had lost just over 300 killed and wounded but the militias had been especially encouraged by their ability to hold ground against the professional soldiers of the British Army and inflict such damage upon them.

Nevertheless, if Burgoyne had immediately followed up the exhausted Americans with his remaining reserve troops, it is likely that the British could have overrun the American position on Bemis Heights, for after the intense fighting at Freeman's Farm the rebels had scarcely any ammunition left. Fraser and Riedesel had urged Burgoyne to press on, but Burgoyne, conscious of the great losses that his forces had sustained, decided to dig in and hold his position around Freeman's Farm, from where he still hoped to be able to bombard the American positions on Bemis Heights. His uncharacteristic decision to move from an offensive to a defensive strategy seemed to be justified two days later when he received a message from General Clinton in New York. This informed him that Clinton intended to despatch a relief force up the Hudson River to take Fort Montgomery. It was due to arrive there on 22 September, assuming that it was not held up en route. Burgoyne could therefore expect this force to launch an attack on Albany to his south in ten days' time. This would hopefully draw the rebels away from Saratoga. At the same time, Burgoyne heard that a rebel force had captured forts Edward and George to his rear, which meant that he was now effectively besieged in a hostile country by a rebel army that was growing stronger as each day passed. There was to be no going back.

Although to his subordinates he maintained a confident manner, stating that 'this Army will not retreat', Burgoyne had by now essentially lost his offensive spirit. Already conscious of impending disaster, and in an attempt to convince others that it would not be his fault if the advance to Albany ended in defeat, he had written from Fort Edward in August, 'Had I latitude in my orders, I should think it my duty to wait in this position . . . I little for saw that I was to be left to pursue my way through such a tract of country, hosts of foes, without any cooperation from New York.' As far as he was concerned the specific nature of his orders from Lord Germain gave him no option other than to make for Albany. His decision to press on in the absence of any reliable support from the south shows that he had effectively abdicated his command responsibilities, which were, as they still remain for any military commander today, to adjust the original design for battle in the face of changing circumstances. By the end of September, it is clear that Burgoyne was no longer able to cope mentally with the harsh realities of his deteriorating situation. He had become as preoccupied with how to preserve his reputation as he was with how he was going to save his army.

All Gates now needed to do was to wait for Burgoyne to make his last 'one rash Stroke' and victory would be his. For the next two and a half weeks he therefore contented himself with continually harassing the British foraging parties and sniping at their positions. Meanwhile, the British were suffering considerable attrition from the enemy, desertion and sickness. They were short of rations and, most damaging of all, they were extremely short of sleep as a result of the constant attacks by the rebels. Their only dwindling hope was that Clinton would somehow be able to rescue them. It seemed to Burgoyne that this miracle might indeed finally happen when he received a message from Clinton telling him that he had captured forts Clinton and Montgomery located on the Hudson River a week's march away and that there was now 'nothing now between us and Gates . . .'

On 4 October, Burgoyne therefore convened a council of war. To advance or retreat was the question. Riedesel and Fraser argued strongly for a withdrawal to the north into an old defensive position, which could not only be strongly defended, but would also allow the British to reopen their supply lines to Canada. *In extremis*, the British could retreat from this position into Canada before the onset of winter. Burgoyne, however, decided against this course of action, arguing that retreat would remove all pressure on the Americans from the north and so allow Gates to join forces with Washington. Howe would not be able to withstand an attack by such a large combined army and defeat would spell the end of British rule in North America. He decided belatedly to attack, despite the fact that the rebels were now far stronger than him, both numerically and in terms of morale.

This was the bad decision of a bad gambler who risks everything on one last throw. Burgoyne made things even worse by deciding first to launch a reconnaissance of the American position. On 7 October 1777, leaving only 800 men to guard the camp, he set forth on what he called an armed reconnaissance with 1,500 men accompanied by ten pieces of artillery. His objective was to discover the location of the right wing of the enemy. Fraser commanded on the right, Riedesel was in the centre, with Major Acland on the left with companies of British grenadiers. The Americans were quickly alerted to this movement and immediately realized that both flanks of the advancing British troops lay unguarded in the forest. Gates's plan of attack therefore consisted of sending Morgan's riflemen to seize some high ground to the west from where he would be able to bring enfilade fire down on Fraser. At the same time, General

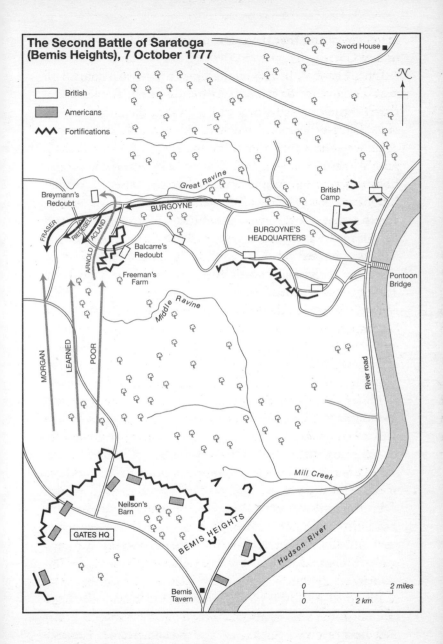

The Second Battle of Saratoga
(Bemis Heights), 7 October 1777

British

Americans

Fortifications

Sword House

Great Ravine

Breymann's
Redoubt

BURGOYNE

British
Camp

FRASER

RIEDESEL

ACLAND

BURGOYNE'S
HEADQUARTERS

ARNOLD

Balcarre's
Redoubt

Freeman's
Farm

Middle Ravine

Pontoon
Bridge

MORGAN

LEARNED

POOR

River road

Mill Creek

Neilson's
Barn

BEMIS HEIGHTS

GATES HQ

Hudson River

Bemis
Tavern

0   2 miles

0   2 km

Poor was to attack Acland on the left while General Learned was to launch an attack on the centre once both flanks had been engaged. Arnold, who had previously quarrelled with Gates, was to be left out of the battle. The odds were four to one in favour of the Americans.

At half past two the battle commenced with Poor attacking Acland so strongly that he was compelled to fall back. On the British right, Morgan attacked Balcarre's light companies. Once again he was obliged to retreat. This left the centre exposed. At a critical moment in the battle, which had lasted no more than half an hour, all the British artillery was captured. Brigadier General Fraser was shortly afterwards killed on direct orders of Daniel Morgan by a rebel sniper called Timothy Murphy, who was able to hit Fraser in the stomach after two failed attempts. Two and a quarter centuries later, such a deliberate targeting of officers by snipers became such a favoured tactic of Iraqi snipers that some American officers in Iraq today refuse to wear their badges of rank.

Meanwhile, the Germans on the British side were still holding two strong positions in the centre – Balcarre's and Breymann's Redoubts. At a critical moment, when it seemed as if the American attack was losing momentum, Arnold arrived on the scene of battle. Without formal command, he rallied the scattered American troops and mounted an attack on the rear of Breymann's Redoubt. This proved too much for the German troops, who hitherto had been putting up a stout resistance to Morgan's riflemen to their front. They fell back in confusion and this heralded a general retreat back into the relative safety of the British lines.

Of 1,500 men, Burgoyne had lost 176 men killed, 250 wounded and 200 taken prisoner. Brigadier General Fraser had been mortally wounded and Major Acland seriously injured. The American losses were 50 killed and 150 wounded. Gates, who had typically played no personal part in the battle, decided to reorganize his forces after the intense engagement and this allowed Burgoyne, as had been originally suggested by Riedesel and Fraser, to withdraw north to a strong defensive position on the Fishkill Creek, which had been previously occupied by the British during their move south. Three days later Gates caught up with the remnants of the British army and effectively surrounded them. The next day Burgoyne sent a flag of truce to Gates, which led to a convention of surrender being signed on 16 October 1777, allowing 'A free Passage to be granted to the Army under Lieut.-General Burgoyne to Great Britain, on Condition of not serving again in North America during the present Contest.'

On hearing this news, Clinton hastily withdrew from the forts that he had captured on the Hudson River and returned to New York. He had already been ordered by Howe to send 4,000 men as reinforcements to Philadelphia, commenting sourly, 'for what purpose, after all the victories we have heard of, he best knows'.

So ended the British attempt to cut off the New England rebels from the southern colonies. By trying to carry out two separate campaigns at the same time, Burgoyne and Howe had succeeded in losing the entire war. Within five months France had signed a treaty with the rebellious Americans, and Britain and France had now become engaged in a world war.

Although Washington had not been present at the battle of Saratoga, he had early on realized that by drawing Burgoyne south he could isolate and degrade his forces. At a point of his choosing, when the balance of force had changed in his favour, he could then destroy them. Therefore, although still threatened by Howe and Clinton in the south, he had reinforced Gates's army at a critical moment – most notably with Arnold and Morgan, both of whom were to play critically important parts in the two battles.

Overall, the blame for the disaster must lie with George III and the British government. They had attempted to plan and direct operations in detail at long distance without knowledge of the facts on the ground. They had not developed a strategy that was consistent with the limited resources that they had made available to the generals in North America, and of course they had remained in denial for far too long about the painful realities of the situation on the ground. They had greatly underestimated their opponents' ability to rapidly concentrate their forces. As Carleton put it after Saratoga, 'This unfortunate event will in future prevent Ministers from pretending to direct operations of war in a country at three thousand miles distance of which they have so little knowledge as not to be able to distinguish between good and bad, or interested advices, or to give positive orders upon matters which, from their nature, are ever on the change.'

One suspects that the British government's strategic failings in North America resonate with modern American commanders in Iraq. For they have been committed to a similarly unwinnable war and are also having to deal with tactical-level interference from their political masters back in Washington DC, who can nowadays see in real time events unfolding on the battlefield, but of course remain none the wiser regarding the tactical decisions that need to be taken on the ground.

Chapter Four

You cannot conquer America.   LORD CHATHAM

The defeat of Washington at Germantown in October 1777 marked a low point in the rebels' fortunes, coming so soon after their defeat at Brandywine. Apart from Trenton and Princeton, Washington's record against the British had been one of continuous defeat and this compared badly with Gates's victory over Burgoyne at Saratoga. The growing criticism in Congress of Washington's defensive strategy led to calls within Congress and the military for his replacement by Horatio Gates. Lovell, who was chairman of the Congress committee for foreign affairs, had even told Gates that 'if it were not for the defeat of Burgoyne and the strong appearance of European War, our affairs are Fabiused into a very disagreeable posture'. By this he meant that Washington had mistakenly decided upon a defensive rather than offensive strategy.

However, the criticisms coming from Congress failed to recognize the key fact that the Continental Army that was by now located at Valley Forge close to Philadelphia, was in no position to take on the main part of the British Army during the winter of 1777. By then its numbers had dwindled to 3,000 men, it lacked adequate clothing and rations, and was desperately short of ammunition. A winter campaign was out of the question. 'All my men except eighteen are unfit for duty for want of shoes, stockings and shirt breeches and coats . . . we are becoming exceedingly lousy,' wrote one battalion commander. Another reported that his men were 'so naked they were ashamed to be seen'. Indeed, some soldiers in the Continental Army had mutinied over their poor conditions. It was clear to Washington and his officers that, before he could once again take to the battlefield, he had to completely rebuild his forces. A regular system was urgently needed for the raising, training, equipping and, above all, paying of the soldiers.

Washington had already warned Congress of the dire situation facing him: 'I do not know from what cause this alarming deficiency or rather total failure of supplies arises, but unless more vigorous exertions and better regulations take place in that line, immediately, the army must dissolve . . . had a body of the enemy crossed the Schuylkill this morning as I had reason to expect, the divisions which I ordered to be in readiness to march and meet them, could not have been moved.' It was also important that the Continental Army should now become entirely independent of the state militias, whose limited terms of service and frequent refusal to accept the authority of Congress always made them too unreliable as a source of recruits. Indeed, the day before the first battle of Saratoga, Stark, the hero of Bennington, had marched his 600 soldiers off the battlefield at midnight, declaring that their two months' service was up and his men were going home – regardless of the consequences. Urgent action was needed by both Congress and Washington if the body and soul of the rebellion was to be kept alive.

Howe's failure to follow up his successes against the rebels at Brandywine and Germantown gave Washington the chance to reconstitute his army. Throughout the winter of 1777 he set about drilling and training his men. He was greatly helped by a number of foreign volunteer officers, including most notably the Prussian Baron von Steuben, who had arrived at Valley Forge with a letter of introduction from Benjamin Franklin describing him as 'a Lieut.Genl. in the king of Prussia's service'. In fact, he was an out-of-work former captain of the Prussian Army. However, he had a good understanding of the military art and, although he spoke little English, was instrumental in drilling and training the American soldiers in the European style. To simplify the procedures that had to be carried out on the battlefield, he rewrote the standard manual of drills for the army and reduced the number of commands that had to be learned from twenty-one to ten. At the same time, Washington tightened up discipline and introduced new regulations covering everything from dress regulations to hygiene. With the support of the French and Dutch, a new line of supplies was opened up via the Dutch West Indies, in spite of the Royal Navy's efforts to halt this flow of war material. By May 1778, the strength of the rebel army had reached 11,800 men. Much new equipment had arrived, including uniforms, weapons and ammunition. This, combined with the rebels' growing experience of the operational level of war, enabled Washington for the first time to compete on equal terms with Howe. The strategic balance had started to swing in favour of the Americans.

Had the British been able to successfully blockade the thirteen rebellious colonies using maritime power, the rebels' combat power would have been so seriously reduced that it would have been impossible for them to win the war. As it was, the increasing delivery of military supplies and reinforcements to the rebels turned the balance against the British, and defeat for them became inevitable.

Today there has been a significant flow of money, men

and material to support the insurgency into Iraq, which the US has similarly been unable to stem. This has come mainly from Syria and Iran, and also from millions of individual Islamic sympathizers around the world who are appalled by the presence of foreigners in a country where some of the most holy sites of Islam, after Mecca and Medina, are located. Having begun the insurgency in 2003 with weapons and ammunition taken from Saddam Hussein's old armouries, within a couple of years the insurgents were able to take advantage of advanced technology coming from abroad. The most important of the new weapons has been the simple but effective anti-armour roadside bomb, which is triggered by the breaking of an infra red beam. The lethal nature of this weapon system has greatly reduced the flexibility and mobility of the occupation forces, and forced them to radically change their methods of operation. This has made it extremely difficult for them to maintain a routine presence amongst the Iraqi civilian community and it has limited the level of support that they can give to the Iraqi security forces. It has also prevented civil contractors from making progress in the reconstruction of Iraq. A task force has been set up and millions of dollars have been expended in the search for a counter to the roadside bomb, but after four years of war these efforts had proved to be of no avail. The strategic consequences of the introduction of this simple piece of new technology have been far-reaching. It has been a classic example of asymmetric warfare.

Howe and his headquarters, like the later American administration securely installed in the Green Zone in Baghdad, had spent the winter of 1777 comfortably garrisoned in Philadelphia, isolated from the mass of the American colonists and insulated from the unpleasant realities of the developing situation on the ground. Their comfortable life was a far remove from the difficult conditions being experienced by the rebels a few miles down the road at Valley Forge. During the winter Howe made no serious effort to hunt down and destroy the remnants of Washington's army, possibly because he had lost any enthusiasm that he might once have had for the war. Howe had already demanded to be recalled to London, disillusioned by the lack of material support that he had received and the fact that his advice about the conduct of the war had been generally ignored. Meanwhile, he was quite happy to remain in Philadelphia – dividing his time between dining out, going to the theatre and regularly visiting his mistress, who was the wife of a commissary of prisoners. A contemporary American rebel song accurately summed up his contribution as commander-in-chief that winter:

> Sir William, he, as snug as a flea
> Lay all this time a-snoring
> Nor dreamed of harm, as he lay warm
> In bed with Mrs Loring.

On 8 May 1778, Howe handed over his command to Henry Clinton. On his return to England he was applauded by the House of Commons for having won so many battles against George Washington. It seems to have escaped the MPs' attention that after three years of effort, Britain was actually losing the war in North America owing to the many strategic failures over which Howe had presided. He ultimately retired from the army in the rank of full general. Even if the politicians of the day had privately understood his strategic failure, they would have had too much to lose themselves by any attempt publicly to disgrace him – for he would have, with some credibility, been able to divert much of the blame for the failures of the war onto George III and the British government. Certainly there was, at that time, no strong pressure in the British Parliament to question the conduct of the war by the Lord North administration or, indeed, to call for an end to the war. There had, however, been a recognition that the original political aims of the war would have to be modified as it was obvious by then that it would not be possible to crush the rebellion by military force. Lord North had consequently agreed that a peace commission should be sent to America to end the war. Britain was now prepared to renounce any right to tax Americans, although trade would continue to be regulated. Any demand for complete independence, however, would be firmly rejected by the peace commissioners, who were described by Horace Walpole as being 'fit to make a treaty that will not be made'. He had already understood that independence was now the only political condition acceptable to the rebels.

Until the mid term US elections held on 7 November 2006 when the Democrats gained an overall majority in both houses, years after the start of the war in Iraq, an identical reluctance to question the conduct and aims of the war was still being demonstrated by members of the US Congress – the majority of whom, of course, originally supported the invasion of Iraq. Although in 2003 it was clear that the Bush administration was taking America on a disastrous course, few spoke up against the war. Many politicians were too frightened, like the British Whigs, of being accused of being unpatriotic if they criticized the war. Like the British parliamentarians of the eighteenth century, it seems that they preferred to see more soldiers lose their lives than risk their reputations.

In London, Lord North and Germain realized that the defeat of Burgoyne at Saratoga made it inevitable that

France would enter the war. They therefore issued Clinton with new orders on 8 March 1778, laying down a new strategy for the reduction of the American rebels. Clinton was ordered to concentrate his forces in New York, even if the consequences of this meant the evacuation of Philadelphia. Clinton was to cease major land operations against Washington in the northern colonies and limit any offensive action there to small raids on rebel-held ports along the coastline. Troops being sent from England that had been destined for New York would now be sent to the British garrisons in Halifax and the West Indies in case of French attack. Clinton would receive less than 4,000 troop reinforcements, even though the commander of the army in England, Lord Amherst, had estimated ten times that number would be needed for the conquest of America. In the autumn Clinton was to launch a limited military offensive into the southern colonies where the rebels were militarily weak and where it was believed a large number of loyalists were waiting to fight for the King. In developing this new southern-based strategy it was assumed that a sizeable majority of the three-quarters of a million white settlers and most of the large slave population in the south would side with the British. British troops would therefore easily deal with the rebel militia in the southern colonies. Once Georgia and Southern Carolina had been seized, it would then be simple to take Virginia from the south and isolate Washington in the middle colonies. North Carolina was, after all, merely 'the road to Virginia', where Germain believed 'a large number of inhabitants would flock to the King's standard and that His Majesty's Government would be restored in that province also'.

Self-delusion is frequently a characteristic of politicians desperate to prop up their failing policies, and Lord North and Germain were no exception in making such fatally flawed assumptions. A similarly flawed assumption was, of course, made by the Bush administration about the support that the Americans would get from the Iraqis after the overthrow of Saddam Hussein. The consequence of this is also likely to be a collapse of Bush's entire forward strategy for fighting global terrorism in the Middle East. Before any southern campaign could take place in 1778, Clinton first had to withdraw to New York, where he could concentrate the main part of his forces. This, he hoped, would give him better strategic balance. Lacking adequate means to evacuate Philadelphia by sea, Clinton decided to make the retreat overland to New York. This was a difficult and hazardous undertaking, given the 60 miles of hostile country that he would have to cross with 15,000 men accompanied by a large baggage train. He set off on 18 June 1778.

Washington's spies had kept him well briefed on the British plans and he sent small parties to destroy the bridges along Clinton's route. He ordered Gates to advance south down the Hudson River to head him off from the north, while he followed a parallel route on Clinton's left flank. His design of battle, in accordance with his newly adopted principle of insurgency warfare, was not to force Clinton into a fixed battle, but to harass him and impose a high level of attrition from the flanks.

After ten days' difficult march, Clinton's forces found themselves strung out over a 12-mile distance. Washington therefore decided to mount a sizeable attack on the rear echelons of the retreating army, giving command to General Charles Lee, who had recently been released by the British in an exchange of prisoners. The two sides met at dawn on the morning of 28 June 1778 at a place called Monmouth Court House.

Because of some confusion about the precise whereabouts of the British echelons, Lee delayed his main attack until ten o'clock, which the British cavalry were easily able to repulse. On hearing the firing, Clinton immediately sent strong reinforcements to his rear and the Americans fell back without putting up significant resistance. Washington rode up and after a terse exchange with Lee, took personal command of the rebel force and ordered the retreating soldiers to march back towards the advancing British and resume the attack. However, the chances of achieving a major blow against the British had been lost by the indecisive behaviour of Lee. When the fighting finally ended at last light, neither side had gained a decisive victory, and the next morning Clinton was able to resume his withdrawal without interruption. In spite of the uncalled-for retreat by Lee, the battle of Monmouth Court House had proved to be a useful demonstration of the success of Washington's new insurgent strategy of advancing when the enemy retreated. Although the Americans had lost 450 killed and wounded in the battle, the British had suffered nearly 1,200 casualties, which they could ill afford to lose.

By the summer of 1778, Clinton's overall strategic situation was not looking as balanced as he had hoped, in spite of his abandonment of Philadelphia and the concentration of the main part of his land forces in New York. Although the rebel army in North America was growing daily stronger, he was still under orders to detach 5,000 troops and artillery for the invasion of St Lucia and also send 3,000 more men to reinforce the British presence in Florida.

With the entry of France into the war, what had been a limited colonial insurrection had now turned into a land and sea war. The centre of gravity of this war, for the British, now lay to the south in the West Indies, not in North America. The resulting diversion of naval support, men and material away from the North American theatre of operations meant that Clinton had little hope of ever gaining the strategic advantage or being able to take the initiative against Washington. For without naval superiority he could no longer move his land forces by sea or supply them at will.

The traditional strategy of the British Navy had usually consisted of blockading the French fleets in their own ports, but the significant increase in size of the French fleet made this difficult to achieve with any degree of certainty. There was every chance that a French naval force would now be able to escape the British blockade in the Channel and Mediterranean and subsequently threaten the North American coastline. If this happened, Britain's only response was to send a detachment from the home fleet to hunt the French down and attempt to bring them to battle before they reached North America. The vastness of the North Atlantic and the frequent ocean storms that arose, even in summer, made this akin to looking for a needle in a haystack. It was clear that from now on Clinton could no longer rely on permanent British naval support.

On 5 July 1778, Clinton's worst fears became a reality: three days after he arrived back in New York from Philadelphia, a large French fleet commanded by Admiral d'Estaing arrived with 4,000 troops at the mouth of the Delaware River – from where it moved north towards New York. Admiral Howe, the brother of the recently departed British commander-in-chief, immediately stationed his ships on the inner side of the sand bar at Sandy Hook at the mouth of the Hudson River. Here the French fleet would have great difficulty in attacking him, as they would have limited manoeuvrability and could easily be engaged by shore batteries.

After refusing battle against Howe, Admiral d'Estaing, who was by then in contact with Washington, received orders to land his French troops on Rhode Island, where a force of 5,000 British troops under General Pigot had been besieged for some time. His mission was to support the American rebels under command of General Sullivan and enable him to capture the entire British garrison – thus repeating the triumph of Saratoga. Washington considered the success of this operation to be so strategically important that he sent generals Nathanael Greene and Lafayette to reinforce Sullivan. It was evident that Pigot could not hold out for long against such a strong combined land and naval force.

Admiral Howe, who had been waiting in vain for naval reinforcements to arrive from England under command of Admiral Byron, felt that he could delay no longer before moving against d'Estaing. Although outgunned by the French, he sailed for Rhode Island, where he arrived on 8 August 1778. Having only just completed the difficult operation of landing 4,000 French troops across the beaches, the sight of British ships to his rear caused d'Estaing to change his plans. He immediately put to sea in order to avoid becoming trapped amongst the shallows that surround Rhode Island. After two days of indecisive engagements in tempestuous weather in which both fleets suffered storm damage, the British and French lost sight of each other. D'Estaing was forced to depart for Boston to repair his fleet and Howe likewise returned to New York to repair damage done to his ships by the storm.

Seeing that they had been so quickly abandoned by the French Navy, many of Sullivan's militiamen lost heart and went home. Sullivan was therefore forced to lift the siege and start a retreat. Pigot immediately gave pursuit and it was only through the spirited action of an all-negro rebel rearguard battalion, who fought a gallant delaying battle against Pigot, that Sullivan was able to escape with his main party back onto the mainland.

On 29 August 1778, as the last American rebel troops crossed to the mainland from Rhode Island, Clinton arrived in Rhode Island with 4,000 troop reinforcements. If he had managed to get there one day earlier, he could have turned the tables on the rebels and captured Sullivan's entire army, thus avenging Burgoyne. However, he had been delayed by a combination of poor weather and his naval commander's reluctance to venture out to sea without reinforcement from across the Atlantic.

The loss of Rhode Island was blamed by many Americans on d'Estaing's sudden departure, and the defeat was to sow seeds of disharmony between the Americans and French. When, shortly after, a French officer was killed in a riot in Boston, relations deteriorated still further. However, the blame was diplomatically put on paroled British soldiers living in that town. Washington subsequently wrote of the French to his military commanders, 'We should remember that they are a people old in war, very strict in military etiquette and apt to take fire where others scarcely seem warmed.' Critically, George Washington had been able to keep his main ally engaged. This is something that his successor George Bush has generally failed to do in Iraq, since most of the nations that were happy to join the Coalition at the start of the war had withdrawn their contingents by 2006. Even Britain which was the largest troop contributor in Iraq after the Americans, had declared 'mission accomplished' in the summer of 2007, and had handed over control of Basra and the four southern provinces to the Iraqis by the end of the year.

Clinton had almost lost Rhode Island because of Admiral Byron's delayed arrival in America. Admiral Byron had, early on in his career, earned the nickname 'Foul Weather Jack' because he always seemed to attract bad weather whenever he set sail. He had left England on 9 June 1778, but typically his ships had been scattered by violent summer storms. It was not until 30 July that his first ship arrived in New York, only just in time to join Howe and help chase d'Estaing away from Rhode Island. This set the pattern for naval support to Clinton, who during the remaining three years of the war was never able to complete a campaign without it being curtailed by the sudden appearance of a French fleet. Whether he liked it or not, Clinton had now been forced into a defensive posture that would ultimately cost Britain the war.

In the short term, however, the withdrawal of the French fleet to Boston did create a temporary window of opportunity for Clinton. Although desperately short of naval and military resources, he believed that by adopting a carefully phased plan it would still be possible to crush the rebellion in North America. He wrote at the time that 'to force Washington to an action upon terms tolerably equal has been the object of every campaign during this war'.

To accomplish this he would first open a southern campaign, which Germain had long been pressing him to do. Germain wrote to Clinton, 'The recovery of the southern provinces, and the prosecution of the war by pushing our conquests from south to north, is to be considered as the chief and principal object of all the forces under your command.' Secondly, he would mount harassing raids on the rebel seaports in order to disperse Washington's defences. Finally, he would force Washington into battle by advancing north into the Highlands, so threatening once again to cut off New England from New Jersey and the southern colonies.

Washington, well aware of the different options open to the British, decided to establish a chain of defensive positions in a wide circle around New York. These stretched from Danbury in the north to Middlebrook in the south.

From these secure bases he would continue to threaten Clinton's own base and headquarters in New York. In the south, Washington would keep only a limited force under General Robert Howe of 700 regular Continental soldiers and 150 militiamen. Their mission was to defend the southern borders of Georgia against British raids from East Florida. However, after a successful raid against the British in East Florida, Howe was able to recruit additional soldiers to the rebel cause and this increased his numbers to a total of 1,500 men.

In November 1778, Clinton opened the southern campaign by ordering General Augustine Prevost in East Florida to capture the important port of Savannah in the neighbouring state of Georgia. Prevost was to move overland and join forces with an expeditionary force of 3,500 men that was being sent from New York under Lieutenant Colonel Campbell. Another small force of Indians was to threaten Savannah by land from the north. On receiving news of Prevost's approach from the south, the American rebel commander General Howe was compelled to send half his force to block Prevost. This left him with less than 700 troops to defend Savannah from the sea. On learning from local people that he was opposed by such a small force, Campbell decided not to wait for Prevost to arrive. On 29 December 1778, he sent a column of Highlanders and light infantry through the swamps that surrounded Savannah to bypass the rebel defences. Using a hidden path, the soldiers were soon able to outflank the enemy defences, and at three o'clock in the afternoon they launched a surprise attack from the north. Meanwhile, Campbell kept the rebels occupied with artillery fire from the expected direction of attack. The rebels' left flank quickly collapsed and the British were able to enter the town without further resistance. The Americans suffered 80 men killed and 500 captured, while the British casualties numbered no more than 26 killed or wounded. All resistance in Georgia collapsed and Colonel Campbell subsequently claimed to be 'the first officer . . . to take a stripe and star from the rebel flag of Congress'.

The way now lay open for Clinton to seize the great prize of the port of Charleston, which lay 100 miles to the north. But it was a prize that was to lie unclaimed for another year, for Clinton was determined to move against Charleston only when every military asset available to him was in place. When developing the plan to take Charleston, he was much encouraged by a letter that he had received the year before from the British governor of Florida saying, 'I am certain that the four southern provinces are incapable of making any very formidable resistance; they are not prepared for a scene of war.' General Prevost, writing from East Florida, had also reinforced Clinton's optimism by telling him that the fall of Charleston would be 'a blow to the rebellious colonies from which they could not recover and which might reduce them to reason much sooner than anything that can be effected to the northward'.

In the meantime, on 5 May 1779 he set the second phase of the Germain plan into operation in which coastal depots of the rebels were to be raided. An army commanded by General Mathew was accordingly landed at Portsmouth in Chesapeake Bay, where the local population proved to be surprisingly friendly. Mathew was able to destroy a large amount of rebel supplies without serious opposition before re-embarking. Encouraged by this success, two weeks later, on 30 May 1779, Clinton seized two rebel forts at Stony Point and Verplanck on either side of the Hudson, which guarded the main line of supply between New England and New Jersey. Loss of these forts meant that the rebels would now have to take a much longer 90-mile route via the

Highlands to the north to maintain their lines of communication. Pressure from Congress was mounting on Washington to respond to Clinton's moves.

Washington, in accordance with his guerrilla tactics, did not respond to these attacks by Clinton directly. He first reinforced General Putnam at West Point to block any moves further north by Clinton and he then instructed one of his best officers, General Wayne, to recover the forts that had been captured. Fortunately for the rebels, Clinton had already returned to New York with his main force, not wishing to deplete the defences of his main base for too long. He had therefore only left a small garrison force behind in each fort.

Back in New York, in spite of the tactical successes that he had so far achieved in his three-phase operational plan, Clinton was becoming increasingly frustrated by his inability to bring Washington to decisive battle, gloomily predicting that 'Another year's expense of this destructive war was now going to be added to the four which had so unprofitably preceded, without a probability of its producing a single event to better our condition or brighten our prospects.'

To fill time, Clinton mounted small but savage raids into New England at Norwalk, New Haven and Fairfield under command of General Tryon, who had formerly been governor of New York. Before that, he had been royal governor of North Carolina, where he had crushed the so-called 'Regulator Rebellion' with a great deal of savagery. He was a determined advocate of the tactics of terror. During the Revolutionary War, the people of Fairfield had found themselves in a particularly difficult position. They were strong patriots but their town was located in a predominantly Tory area of Connecticut. On the morning of

7 July 1779, approximately 2,000 British troops landed on Fairfield beach and attacked the town. When they left the following evening, the entire town lay in ruins. Its churches and houses had all been burned to the ground in what Tryon regarded as a punishment for the people of Fairfield's support of the rebel cause. When passing through the town ten years later, President George Washington observed that 'the destructive evidences of British cruelty are yet visible both in Norwalk and Fairfield; as there are the chimneys of many burnt houses standing in them yet'.

Clinton was so fearful about the great damage done by these raids that he wrote a sharp note to Tryon stating that the level of force used had been against his express orders. Clinton was worried about the effect of these atrocities not only on local American support for the British, but also on public opinion at home. Such acts would inevitably strengthen the hand of the anti-war lobby and weaken that of the government. The sort of punitive action carried out by Tryon in Connecticut has, throughout history, been the classic reaction of an occupation force unable to bring insurgents to battle. The result of such actions has always been to alienate the local population, and the raids in Connecticut were no exception.

At the start of any insurgency, a civilian population is usually divided into one-third that supports the armed struggle, one-third that supports the government and one-third that remains uncommitted to either side. If the government forces cannot mobilize the support of the last-mentioned group then it will surely lose the war, for the uncommitted will ultimately be forced to take sides with the insurgents. Even those who initially supported the side of the government will inevitably have to abandon it.

The difficulty facing the Americans in the spring of

2004 was typical for those attempting to win a counter-insurgency war. How to persuade an uncommitted civilian population to give their support to the government forces while at the same time hunting down and destroying the many insurgents who were already established in their midst? Too overt and oppressive a military presence and the people would turn against the foreign occupier. Too little and the insurgents would take control. This was the problem faced both by generals Howe and Clinton in North America in the eighteenth century and by General Sanchez, the commander of the Coalition forces in Iraq, two and a quarter centuries later.

The problem was particularly acute in Fallujah, given the deep hostility that many local people felt towards the West. During the first Gulf War in 1991, an RAF Tornado aircraft had dropped a bomb on a crowded market place in Fallujah and this had killed 130 Iraqis and wounded many others. Following the invasion of Iraq in April 2003, soldiers of the 82nd Airborne Division had fired on a crowd outside a school, killing at least seventeen civilians and wounding a further sixty. Later a local police patrol, trained by the Coalition forces, had been fired upon by the Americans and eight policemen had been killed.

Even without these incidents there would have been little support for the Coalition forces. The people of Fallujah are predominantly Sunnis and come from the Dulaimi tribe. Over the centuries the Dulaimis have traditionally wielded considerable power throughout Iraq because of their hold on the army and internal security services. This was true even during the rule of Saddam Hussein. Because of the introduction of a Western democratic system in Iraq, the Dulaimis were likely to lose everything, as power would now inevitably pass to the Shia. Furthermore, Fallujah, which is known as the city of mosques, has strong religious traditions. This also made it likely that the presence in the city of so many foreign infidels would not be tolerated for long. Thus the political, religious and security environment facing the Americans in the spring of 2004 could not have been more awkward. In some respects the arrival of eighteenth-century British troops in Boston in response to the unrest in that city brought about a similar reaction from the radical element. They had become used to running things their own way and the reimposition of British rule by military force caused many people to side with the rebels.

As the insurgency escalated throughout Iraq in 2004, the Americans came to regard Fallujah as a major centre of resistance. They believed that the insurgents located in Fallujah were responsible for the spread of much of the violence that was occurring in Anbar province. On 24 March 2004, the 82nd Airborne Division, which had hitherto deliberately maintained only a light presence in the city in order to avoid stirring up trouble, handed over responsibility for Fallujah to the US Marines.

Shortly after their arrival and in response to a number of attacks against their patrols, a decision was taken by the Marines to enter the city in force. This resulted in a brief but vicious series of firefights, in which fifteen Iraqis were killed and many others wounded. Shortly afterwards four American civilian contractors, passing through Fallujah, were ambushed in a well-publicized incident in which their bodies were seen on television to have been publicly desecrated. This finally convinced the US administration in Washington that something must be done to drive the insurgents from Fallujah and thereby establish full military control of the city. However, the US Marine commander General Mattis was anxious that the Americans should not rush in and so fall into a public relations trap set by the Iraqi insurgents. Too hasty and oppressive an American response would risk heavy civilian losses and cause great damage to the city. A more measured approach would produce a better result in time. But Washington was adamant. The inhabitants of Fallujah were to be taught a lesson. There was to be no delay.

General Mattis's worst fears were unfortunately realized when Operation Vigilant Resolve was launched on 5 April 2004. Up to 1,200 heavily armed insurgents were waiting for the Marines in well-prepared positions – many of them located in civilian houses, schools and mosques. In the words of a Marine post-action report, the enemy 'manoeuvred effectively, and stood and fought'. On 5 April – the same day that the Marines had launched their first assault into Fallujah – Paul Bremer, in a classic example of bad timing, had issued a warrant for the arrest of an important Shia leader, Moqtada al-Sadr. This had resulted in a doomsday situation in which the multinational forces had had to deal with Sunni and Shia rebellions simultaneously. The Shia Sadr militias had gained control of many Iraqi cities including Kufa, Najaf, Basra and Sadr City. In the following weeks, tanks, artillery and air strikes were used in built-up areas to support the three US Marine battalions that were forced to fight from house to house against the unexpectedly strong opposition. By 8 April, General Sanchez, the senior commander on the ground in Iraq, reported 'tremendous progress in restoring legitimate authority to Fallujah'. But if the tactical battle in Fallujah was indeed being won, the information battle was being substantially lost. Television images of dead and wounded civilians and thousands of refugees fleeing from their homes were shown around the world. This caused even Washington to rethink its strategy and negotiations were opened with the insurgents via the pro-insurgent city council. After a number of ceasefire violations by the insurgents, who felt that each day they

fought on would bring them greater popular support, a halt
to the fighting was finally agreed. It was also accepted by
both sides that an ad hoc Iraqi brigade, made up of former
members of the Iraqi Army, should be interposed between
the insurgents and the Americans. The first battle for Fallujah had lasted less than a month and it had been a public
relations disaster.

The withdrawal of the Marines from Fallujah was hailed
by the insurgents as a clear defeat for the Americans and
dramatic proof that the resistance could prevail. Although
peace did return, the insurgents remained in full control of
the city and they soon resumed their brutal intimidation of
the inhabitants of Fallujah and the exporting of violence
throughout Anbar province and elsewhere. The Americans
had not been able to reconcile the need for firm military
action with winning the information battle. They were to
have a second opportunity to do so seven months later
when the second battle for Fallujah began.

By the summer of 2004 the security situation throughout
Iraq had greatly worsened, and things were particularly bad
in Anbar province, where Fallujah was located. Ramadi, the
capital of Anbar province, and Samarra, another major city,
had been lost to the insurgents. By the autumn, attacks
against the Coalition forces had reached over four hundred
a week and the overall situation seemed to be getting out of
control.

In Fallujah the need to deal with the security situation
was once again becoming urgent, especially as it was
suspected that Abu Musab al-Zarqawi, the chief of al-
Qaeda in Iraq, was based in the city. This led to air attacks
being mounted against Fallujah – without noticeably reducing the level of violence. On 27 September, Prime Minister
Iyad Allawi, in an interview on Arab television, indicated
that a 'military option' would have to be adopted if a

political agreement could not be reached to restore Iraqi government control in the city.

In the absence of any response from the insurgents to this threat, the US administration, in conjunction with the Iraqi government, finally decided to make a second decisive military assault on Fallujah. However, on this occasion adequate time would be given to the planning of the operation and sufficient resources would be made available. The fact that applying 'more of the same' in a fast-deteriorating situation rarely brings success seems to have been ignored. A complete rethink of America's policy objectives in Iraq and a reassessment of the methods being used by the military were clearly needed. Such a reappraisal should, of course, have been done by the British government of Lord North after the disaster of Saratoga in 1777. But the British at that time had been as determined as President Bush and his strategic planners were in 2004 that the simple remedy of greater force would bring about victory. Both had been deluded by their own propaganda, which, as events demonstrated, was far removed from reality.

The first problem facing the Americans in autumn 2004 was how to protect the civilian population from what would be extremely intensive fighting. If the civilians fled from the city, that would clear the fields of fire for the attackers. However, too great an exodus and the humanitarian problem might overwhelm the American and Iraqi aid organizations. There would certainly be much negative propaganda if so many people had to leave their homes.

Second, since there was little intelligence available to the Americans concerning the locations, numbers and capabilities of the insurgents in Fallujah, from October 2004 air and artillery strikes and feint moves by ground troops were made against suspected positions. This was done in order to provoke a response that would enable the Americans to identify the true whereabouts of the insurgents and their defensive positions in and around Fallujah. Given the limitations of this approach, however, it was inevitable that the main attack would have to be mounted without sufficient intelligence. It would be impossible to target the insurgents specifically and civilian casualties could therefore be expected.

Thirdly, it was necessary to minimize the public relations damage that would be done to the Iraqi and American governments by what would have to be a massive assault into Fallujah. Given the lack of intelligence and the practice of the insurgents of locating their defensive positions in populated areas, this was the most difficult problem for the Americans to solve. The previous assault on Fallujah had resulted in thousands of Iraqis joining the resistance. The Americans were determined that the same thing would not happen with the second assault. Each action and target would be tested against the criteria of Iraqi acceptability and legality, and Iraqi troops would be integrated into the assault force as much as possible. This assault force consisted of 8,000 US Marines and soldiers supported by 2,000 Iraqis. This was three times the number of troops that had taken part in the first assault on Fallujah. A joint American/ Iraqi command headquarters was established and an Iraqi officer, General Abdul Qader, put in nominal command of the operation. Civil military teams were to closely follow the assaulting units into the city to ensure that humanitarian support was available to the civilian population. Prime Minister Iyad Allawi announced that he had given 'full authority to the multinational and Iraqi forces. We are determined to clean Fallujah from the terrorists.' It is doubtful if more could have been done by the Americans in terms of preparing for the second assault into Fallujah. But the strategic consequences of this second assault would be no less damaging in propoganda terms as those resulting from the first.

In a preliminary action on 7 November, the Fallujah General Hospital was seized by US and Iraqi troops on the outskirts of Fallujah. The building was being used by the insurgents as a headquarters and its capture also closed a main route into the city from the west. Because indirect fire was not used, there was little negative fallout from this action. Medical teams and supplies were quickly brought into the hospital and assistance was given to the existing staff. It had been a good public relations start to the assault. However, the electricity supply was cut to the city to enable the Marines to move without being observed and this had the opposite effect.

Fallujah was now surrounded and cut off from the outside world by the 1st Marine Division, supported by elements of the US and Iraqi armies. The main attack into the city came on 8 November from the north. This was a surprise to the insurgents, who had been persuaded by previous feints that the main assault would come from the south. Progress was at first rapid, but slowed as the Marines reached the main defensive positions of the insurgents in the south of the city. It was later estimated that more than two-thirds of the 300,000 civilians had left the city before the attack began. This made movement for the multinational forces much easier and greatly limited the number of civilian casualties. After three days of intense fighting, the Marines reached the centre of the city and occupied the mayor's office. As the attack progressed, the Marines uncovered gruesome evidence of the atrocities carried out by the extremist insurgents against the civilian population. Over the next ten days the assault forces, using tanks, artillery and air strikes, cleared the remainder of the city. By 15 November, major operations had ended apart from small pockets of resistance. The second battle for Fallujah was over.

It was estimated that up to 1,200 insurgents were killed, although many had left the city before the battle began. It was also reported that seventy-one Americans and eight Iraqis were killed and nearly 600 multinational soldiers injured – most of them Americans. Nevertheless, it had been a textbook example of how to fight in built-up areas – the most difficult and dangerous type of conflict. The US Marines and American soldiers had fought courageously and determinedly, often putting their own lives at risk in order to minimize civilian losses. One Marine commentator estimated that it had been the toughest battle fought by US Marines since the battle for Hue in South Vietnam.

Despite this military triumph, the second assault on Fallujah, like the first, had been an information battle disaster. Two hundred thousand people had been forced to flee from their homes and many civilians had been killed or injured – although it is impossible to verify the precise number. Much of the city had been destroyed, bearing out the determination of one commanding officer who said before the battle that 'there is not going to be one stone unturned in the city'. One reporter likened Fallujah to Stalingrad.

In spite of a massive reconstruction programme, two years later much of Fallujah still remained derelict and empty of people. Nevertheless, the Marine commander, Lieutenant General Sattler, was quoted on 18 November 2004 as saying that the battle for Fallujah had turned the tide in the 'fight against the insurgency in the al Anbar province . . . the insurgents are on the run'. What had actually happened was a group of mostly foreign extremist fighters, who were prepared to die fighting the infidels, had been left behind in Fallujah. The main body of insurgents had simply left the city, along with the civilian population, in order to take the battle elsewhere. Within a year the number of attacks against the multinational forces was running at nearly 700 per week – with Anbar province having one of the highest levels of violence.

The American and Iraqi governments had tried hard before the battle to get the message across that collateral damage would be minimal and the elimination of the insurgents' stronghold in Fallujah would improve the security situation throughout Iraq. However, the reports of destruction and civilian suffering caused by the Americans in Fallujah spread throughout Iraq and the rest of the world. America and the Iraqi government were widely condemned both in Iraq and internationally for what had happened. The intensification of the conflict elsewhere proved yet again how difficult it is to balance the need for military action with the need to tread softly. In retrospect, the destruction of Fallujah in 2004 probably represented as great a strategic disaster for the Americans as the destruction of Fairfield and Newhaven had been for the British during the American War of Independence.

The US have been drawn into the cycle of violence and counter-violence that is a central part of any insurgency. If excessive levels of military force have to be used by the security forces to maintain control and if, as a result, large numbers of civilians are killed, displaced or have their homes destroyed, then the vitally important support of the people will be lost. Given the high levels of force used by the Americans in Iraq since 2003, it should be no surprise that the resistance to the American presence in Iraq has greatly increased – and that disaffection with the West has become so universal amongst Muslims around the world. As was so clearly demonstrated in 2004 by the result of the actions in Fallujah, the entire American concept of operations in Iraq at that time, which was based on the use of heavy military force, was bound to fail. In doctrinal terms, it has become aligned to the policy advocated by George III in 1777 when he advised that greater brutality by the British Army in North America would 'bring the Americans in a temper to accept such terms as may enable the mother country to keep them in order . . . the regaining of their affections is an idle idea, it must be the convincing of them that it is in their interest to submit'.

Chapter Five

Experience, my lord, has too fatally taught us that if
by desultory movements we tempt our friends to rise
and join us and are afterwards obliged to leave
them . . . we leave them to ruin and of course lose
their future confidence.   LORD CORNWALLIS

Although George Washington knew Clinton had decided
to switch the main British effort to the south, in the absence
of the French fleet and without sufficient regular troops
it was clear that the Americans were unable to prevent
the initial British move south. Accordingly, Washington
decided to launch diversionary raids against the British in
the north. On 16 July 1779, in a deadly silent night assault
using only the bayonet, General Anthony Wayne's troops
overran the British garrison at Stony Point near New York.
The British lost 63 killed and 534 captured, for a total loss of
84 Americans. One month later, on August 19, Major 'Light
Horse' Henry Lee, who was the father of the Civil War
general Robert E. Lee, attacked another British fort at
Paulus Hook, also just across the Hudson River from New
York. He attacked with 400 infantry and a troop of dis-
mounted dragoons, and, quickly gaining possession of the
outer fort before dawn, he forced the remaining British
defenders to withdraw into a small redoubt. Having no
time to assault the final redoubt before daybreak, Major Lee

decided to retreat, carrying with him 159 British prisoners. In the battle he lost 2 men killed and 3 men wounded.

While the effect of these raids was tactically insignificant, by demonstrating that the American rebels could still concentrate their forces and mount effective operations wherever they chose, Washington greatly reinforced his psychological advantage over Clinton. 'I am afraid,' wrote Lieutenant Colonel Stuart of his close friend Clinton, 'his temper from these two unlucky blows of fortune, became much soured.'

By the spring of 1780, George Washington felt that he now had enough troops to interrupt Clinton's efforts to regain control of North and South Carolina and therefore sent General Benjamin Lincoln to increase the level of rebel activity against the British in the south. General Lincoln was one of his most dependable and trusted officers. He commanded a small army of 1,500 men and had been able to enlist a further 3,000 local militia. He was also able to call on further support from the patriot militias in the Carolinas and Virginia whenever the need arose. Meanwhile, the British remained under the delusion that only a handful of rebels existed in the south and that the majority of the population supported them. Following the capture of Savannah, General Prevost had established a line of defensive posts along the Savannah River between Savannah and Augusta in order to secure Georgia from the remaining rebels in the north. However, the British simply did not have enough troops to simultaneously garrison their bases, dominate the countryside and carry out offensive operations against the rebels. This lack of manpower gave full freedom of manoeuvre to the insurgents and allowed them to attack the British at any point where they showed weakness.

This situation is not unusual in the history of war, for an occupying power is always confronted by the same three key imperatives: to protect military bases; search out and destroy the enemy; and dominate the country. Nowhere has the urgency of these requirements been better demonstrated than in Iraq. Although massively superior in firepower, the US Army in Iraq was always far too weak in terms of troop numbers and intelligence coverage to be able to carry out all these essential tasks at the same time, even when supported by its allies. Above all, at no stage during Operation Iraqi Freedom has the US-led coalition ever been able to protect the civilian population from the insurgents. From the outset of the war, Rumsfeld, like Lord Germain before him, consistently refused to meet calls to significantly increase US troop numbers in Iraq. After four years of a deteriorating situation, it is probably too late politically to contemplate such a measure, for the majority of Americans not only had lost faith in their administration but were also unlikely to accept the sending of large scale reinforcements to support what by then was increasingly seen as a flawed strategy that was leading to disaster. The 23,000 troops sent to Iraq in 2007, the so-called 'surge', was impossible for the US Army to sustain in the long term. Therefore, whilst dramatically successful in Baghdad, this limited reinforcement was not by itself responsible for the general reductions in the overall level of violence in Iraq. More significant, was the decision by the Americans to align themselves with the Sunni insurgents in Anbar province.

Nevertheless, the stronger military power in any insurgency war can still gain small victories whenever the insurgents assemble together and decide to fight a conventional war. Such an opportunity occurred for the British on 3 March 1779, at a place called Briar Creek on the Savannah River. While withdrawing from the garrison at Augusta, a rebel general, John Ashe, had decided to pursue the retreating British force. The British commander, Colonel

Mark Prevost, had detached 900 men from this force and caught up with the rebels while they were camping beside Briar Creek. Some of the rebels managed to escape, but a large number became trapped. Outnumbered and out-gunned, the rebels fought fiercely until virtually all of them had been killed. In total, 400 rebels either died or were captured, while the British side only lost 16 men killed or wounded.

However, this considerable British success did not represent a serious strategic blow to the rebels, any more than the American success in Fallujah in December 2004 represented a strategic disaster for the insurgents in Iraq, who were soon able to replace their losses without reducing the tempo of their operations. In the same way, within a few days of the disaster, General Lincoln was able to replace the losses and return to the offensive. As long as there remained some hope of ending British rule in North America, and as long as the Continental Army remained in existence, the population always responded to any call by Congress, the states or Washington's generals to provide fighting soldiers in the republican cause – often at very short notice. In contrast, the British remained throughout the war extremely short of manpower.

Meanwhile, a shift in the balance of forces in the south had occurred, yet again, with the arrival of a strong French fleet under command of Admiral d'Estaing. It had earlier sailed from the West Indies and had arrived off Savannah on 1 September 1779 with twenty ships of the line and 5,000 troops. D'Estaing's mission was to mount a coordinated attack on Savannah in conjunction with Lincoln, who was marching south from Charleston. However, without waiting for the arrival of Lincoln's army, d'Estaing anchored off Savannah and landed his troops. Shortly after, he sent an emissary to call on the British garrison to surrender. At that point, Prevost only had a force of 2,200 men with which to defend the city, so he cunningly asked for 24 hours to consider the proposal. This ruse allowed him just enough time to move into Savannah his one remaining unit, which was located at Beaufort, a few miles to the north of the city. This reinforcement enabled him to greatly strengthen his defences and the next day he firmly rejected the renewed French call to surrender. When Lincoln and d'Estaing did belatedly attack Savannah on 9 October 1779, after a long bombardment, the British defences proved too strong and the attack was repulsed with a loss of 900 French and Americans killed or wounded. Not since the battle of Bunker Hill had any side in the war sustained such high casualties. Amid great recrimination between the two allies, d'Estaing raised the siege and sailed away. The way was now open for Clinton to take Charleston.

D'Estaing's departure again gave Clinton a brief naval superiority of sixteen ships of the line against the seven French ships remaining in Rhode Island. Taking advantage of this, Clinton sailed from New York on Boxing Day 1779, taking with him nearly 7,000 men in order to finally execute his plan for the capture of Charleston. However, his fleet was dispersed by bad weather off the treacherous North Carolina coastline: 'Full forty days beating the boisterous ocean, signals of distress from transports and no prospect of amend to it.' Nevertheless, the battered fleet did finally manage to assemble at Savannah by the end of January 1780. Clinton was as determined as ever not to fail for a second time to capture Charleston. He had therefore evacuated the British garrison at Rhode Island in order to increase the strength of his invasion force to 14,000 men. This was a high-risk move as it left New York weakly defended against both land and sea attack.

Clinton had always blamed his naval commander, Sir

Peter Parker, for the failure of the previous British attack on Charleston in June 1776. He therefore took particular care to ensure that all the land and naval elements of the operation were properly coordinated. His plan was extremely complicated and involved an approach from the sea along three different sea routes. So it was not until 1 April 1780 that he landed his army and started to excavate the first parallels of the elaborate siege works that he planned to establish around Charleston. Clinton supervised every aspect of this part of the operation personally, often appearing at three o'clock in the morning to inspect the entrenchments. These lengthy preparations undoubtedly paid off, as his troops were never required to mount a direct assault on the city. After a prolonged siege, Lincoln finally surrendered the city on 12 May 1780. Five thousand American rebels, including General Lincoln, were captured, along with all their artillery and stores. The British had lost 76 men killed and 189 wounded during the months of the siege. Careful preparation and planning coupled with extreme caution had finally paid off for Clinton. However, in spite of the fact that the loss of their army at Charleston represented the biggest defeat of the entire war, the overall strategic balance of forces still lay in favour of the American rebels, particularly as Clinton was soon to receive news that a large French fleet was on its way to America under command of Admiral de Ternay.

Clinton's position was now extremely exposed. The 33,000 troops under his command were spread between Nova Scotia and Bermuda, and only 23,000 were fit for duty. He was about to lose naval superiority once again, and although he was being successful in the south, he had not yet brought Washington to battle.

Most worrying of all was the French presence in Rhode Island, where 5,000 troops had now established a firm base at Newport, and this was protected by a small French fleet anchored in Narragansett Bay. Germain had earlier advised Clinton to abandon the Rhode Island garrison: 'Indeed if in consequence of your withdrawing the troops from thence, the southern colonies are recoverable this winter, the wisdom of the measure will be fully manifested.' Despite this, Clinton now realized that a permanent French base in North America so close to New York posed an unacceptable threat. Not only would he have to keep a large number of troops and ships in New York to defend himself, but his maritime lines of communication were no longer secure. It was now imperative that the French should be ejected from Rhode Island before they could start offensive operations against the British and before any further French naval reinforcements arrived. Clinton therefore returned to New York, where instead of regrouping his forces and launching an attack against Rhode Island, he spent the summer quarrelling with his naval commander, Admiral Arbuthnot, about how to deal with the problem.

The arrival of a small fleet from England under command of Admiral Graves in the middle of July 1780 made the launching of an amphibious operation against Rhode Island not only possible but extremely urgent. This was because the small French garrison there had recently been reinforced by the arrival of Admiral de Ternay, who brought with him ten fighting ships and transports containing 6,000 troops under command of Count de Rochambeau. But in spite of the threat they posed, throughout the summer Clinton continued to argue with Arbuthnot about the best way of recapturing Rhode Island. At one point, Clinton actually moved his troops to Huntington Bay on the north shore of Long Island ready for an attack only to find that Arbuthnot had failed to provide fresh water for the troops on the naval transports. The weather changed and Clinton returned empty-handed to New York. As one naval officer said, the British fleet 'would never see Rhode Island because the General hated the Admiral'.

These proved to be prophetic words: for the remainder of the war the French were able to maintain their base in Rhode Island. Indeed, it was from here that Rochambeau finally marched south to join forces with Washington in the siege of Yorktown. To have allowed the French to keep a bridgehead on the continent of North America in what was considered at the time to be 'the best and noblest harbour in America' proved to be a strategic blunder by Germain and Clinton with far-reaching consequences.

Frustrated also by what he saw as a continuing lack of political support in England, and fed up with his quarrels with Arbuthnot and more recently Cornwallis, Clinton asked for a recall, saying that he had become a mere witness 'of the debility of an army at whose head, had I been unshackled by instructions, I might have indulged expectations ordering serious service to my country'. Germain refused either to accept his resignation or to commit himself to sending major reinforcements. To make matters worse, he sketched out for Clinton an entirely new but hopelessly vague campaign plan that consisted of combining coastal raids with a decisive stroke against Washington. This was sheer delusion on the part of the British government, for without sufficient military resources or adequate naval support neither was possible. In this unsatisfactory situation Clinton was obliged to soldier on in command of an army 'from which everything is expected and from which, without uncommon fortune, no expectation can be answered'. By then, Clinton realized that he was in danger of becoming the commander of a forgotten army scattered along a 3,000-mile coastline.

On the American side, Washington was also preoccupied

with the lack of support that he was receiving from Congress. His main problem was keeping his army together and, indeed, his hopes for victory alive in the face of dire shortages of money and material. He realized that he would have to wait for the French to make their next expedition across the Atlantic before making any major moves against the British. He had hoped to be able to launch combined operations against the British that summer, but his plans had been disappointed: 'Instead of having everything ready to take to the field, we have nothing and instead of having the prospect of a glorious offensive campaign before us, we have a bewildered and gloomy defensive one, unless we should receive a powerful aid of ships, land troops and money from our generous allies.' Nor was it certain that this would be forthcoming, for the French were beginning to question their costly continuing support of the American Revolution. Jacques Necker, the French finance minister, wrote in great secrecy to Lord North in December 1780 putting forward his ideas for a peace in America: 'You desire peace, I desire it also; brought together by a feeling so just and by the similarity of our wishes, why should we not try out, one day, this idea on our political masters?' Both sides were now in a situation of strategic stalemate, and both awaited reinforcements from across the Atlantic. The first to receive these would be in an unassailable position.

In the south, Cornwallis was operating without a clear plan or any support from Clinton. Writing to a fellow officer he asked, 'Now my dear friend, what is our plan? Without one we cannot succeed.' He was about to embark on a long and fruitless operation against the rebels in the Carolinas and Virginia that was to end in the battle of Yorktown and ultimately the final withdrawal of the British from North America.

The Southern Colonies, 1779–81

VIRGINIA
James River
Richmond
Jamestown
Williamsburg
Gloucester
Yorktown
Norfolk
Portsmouth
York River
Chesapeake Bay

River Dan
River Roanoke

Guilford
Hillsborough

NORTH

Salisbury

CAROLINA

King's Mtn.
Charlottetown
Catawba River
Cowpens
Winnsborough
Hobkirk's Hill
Camden
Cape Fear River
Ninety Six
SOUTH
River Peedee
Wilmington
Eutaw Springs
River Santee
Maccamaw
Cape Fear
Augusta
CAROLINA
Georgetown
River Savannah
Charleston
Stono Ferry
Sullivan's Island
and Fort Moultrie
GEORGIA
Beaufort
Port Royal Island
Savannah

0   100 miles
0   150 km

Before he had returned to New York in June 1780 after capturing Charleston, Clinton had ordered Cornwallis to send a force into the interior of South Carolina to destroy all the remaining rebels in that state. Cornwallis therefore had immediately despatched a small force of British light dragoon and mounted infantry, under Lieutenant Colonel Banastre Tarleton, in pursuit of a group of 400 Virginians commanded by a militia colonel, Abraham Buford, who were heading north. They had been marching south to support Lincoln in Charleston but, having heard news of its fall, were now heading for home. By the remarkable feat of covering more than 100 miles in two days, Tarleton managed to catch up with this rebel force and surprise it at a place called Waxhaw in South Carolina on 29 May 1780. Exaggerating the strength of his force, Tarleton called on Buford to surrender. He refused, saying, 'I reject your proposals, and shall defend myself to the last extremity.' Despite his brave words the militia were no match for the British cavalry, who soon overwhelmed them and forced them to surrender. There followed a terrible massacre of the disarmed Americans by the British. Tarleton subsequently claimed that the rebels had fired upon him after the flag of surrender had been raised, saying that 'they refused my terms and I have cut 170 officers and men to pieces'. No American believed him nor does to this day, and the name of Tarleton will live on for ever in that continent as that of a brutal murderer.

Meanwhile, Cornwallis had somehow to garrison the four main British coastal ports as well as his inland bases. These included Augusta and Camden, a number of remote outposts in the interior of South Carolina and an important loyalist stronghold called Ninety Six. All this he had to accomplish with a mere 4,000 men. Much depended on the willingness of the American loyalists to step forward and fight for the Crown. But on 3 June 1780, Clinton issued a proclamation stating that every person who had declared themselves to be a loyalist was required to take an oath of loyalty to the Crown. This had the effect of causing the many people who were neutral, or who had pretended to be loyalists for reasons of convenience, to defect to the rebel side. It was one thing to lie to the British, and another thing altogether to profane the word of God. So devastating was the effect of this proclamation that shortly afterwards Cornwallis wrote, 'There was scarce an inhabitant between the Santee and the Pee Dee that was not in arms against us.'

This disastrous mistake by Clinton enabled insurgent leaders such as Thomas Sumter, Andrew Pickens and Francis Marion, 'the swamp fox', to recruit large numbers of people into their rebel militias. In one notable instance, an entire loyalist regiment was persuaded to defect following Clinton's proclamation. During the ensuing year and a half these militia groups operating behind the British lines as guerrillas were to prove vitally important to the commander of the southern army, General Nathanael Greene.

More than two hundred years later, the American administration was to make similar mistakes when on 16 May 2003 Paul Bremer, head of the Coalition Provisional Authority (CPA), signed CPA Order Number 1, which demanded the de-Ba'athification of the entire Iraqi administration. Total membership of the Ba'athist party membership at that time was about 600,000 to 700,000, and it has been estimated that a tenth of this number subsequently joined the resistance. Whatever the accuracy of that figure, it is clear that the collapse of the administration resulting from Bremer's order plunged Iraq into a state of chaos and disorder from which it has not recovered. Shortly afterwards Order Number 2 was issued, disbanding the Iraqi Army, police and internal security forces. The total numbers involved amounted to nearly half a million men. Since many soldiers and policemen had actually supported the overthrow of Saddam Hussein, they felt as betrayed and aggrieved as their civilian counterparts, and once again a large number decided to join the insurgency. Many senior

officials including General Jay Garner, Bremer's predecessor, strongly argued against these decisions, but the
Bush administration entirely rejected their advice.

In response to the fall of Charleston, Washington had
initially sent his old colleague and rival General Horatio
Gates with 2,000 men to reinforce the militias in the south.
Gates's first objective was to capture the British base at
Camden, which he believed was weakly held. Although
Cornwallis was not yet ready to begin his military campaign
to take control of the Carolinas, he could not afford to
abandon Camden to the rebels as it contained great quantities of military stores and 800 sick soldiers. He therefore
set out from Charleston with only a limited force of 1,500
men, some of whom were loyalist militia, in order to block
Gates's advance. At two o'clock in the morning of the 16
August 1780 the two armies met by accident on a road
near Camden. The road was bounded by swamps on both
sides. Both commanders immediately formed their forces
into battle array and at dawn Gates ordered his militia to
attack the British right flank. The American attack was
half-hearted and easily repulsed. The British immediately
counterattacked and at this early moment in the battle the
American militia soldiers, forming what was the American
left flank, threw down their arms and ran away. The better
disciplined British, instead of giving pursuit, wheeled in
the opposite direction and assaulted the flanks of Gates's
main position, which was held by regular troops of the
Continental Army. While Gates's army was engaged from
the front, Tarleton had manoeuvred his cavalry unseen to
the rear from where he launched a surprise attack. This
proved to be too much for the entire American force, who
broke ranks and fled. One thousand rebels were either killed
or wounded and another thousand were taken prisoner.
Abandoning his command, in a hasty flight northwards, it

is claimed that Gates covered 200 miles in two days, enabling him to escape from Tarleton. But the total defeat of the Americans at Camden and Gates's subsequent panicked response effectively ended any chance that he had of replacing Washington as commander-in-chief. Tarleton went on to surprise one of the rebel commanders, Thomas Sumter, and a group of rebel soldiers in a camp at Fishing Creek two days after the battle of Camden – killing or capturing 500 of them. Resistance to the British in South Carolina collapsed.

Buoyed by this success, and wishing to keep the rebels under continuing pressure, Cornwallis abandoned his plans to wait for further reinforcements before launching his major offensive and immediately headed north into North Carolina. Like Germain and Clinton, he firmly but mistakenly believed that there were a significant number of loyalists waiting to rise up in North Carolina in support of the British. However, this expected loyalist uprising did not materialize. Indeed, the further Cornwallis advanced into the difficult back country of the Carolinas, the greater became the resistance from the rebels. Significantly, guerrilla operations also started up again to his rear in South Carolina in areas that he believed had already been pacified.

This heightened rebel activity caused the provincial commander of South Carolina, Major Patrick Ferguson, to issue another proclamation stating that anyone who opposed the British would be hunted down and hanged, and that the countryside would be laid to waste. Since it is a natural instinct of people to defend their homes whatever their political persuasion, the proclamation proved to have negative consequences for the British. Even more people joined the rebel cause and Ferguson's force, which consisted of 1,000 American loyalists, found itself coming under increasing attack. Ferguson had already left his base at Ninety Six, deep in the interior of South Carolina, sensing that he was becoming dangerously isolated. He decided therefore to march across country and join forces with Cornwallis, who was only 35 miles away at Charlottetown. The rebels opposing him, many of whom were frontiersmen from across the border in Tennessee, immediately set off behind him in pursuit. At a place called King's Mountain, Ferguson halted his retreat in order to confront his pursuers, having taken up a defensive position on a high plateau that he believed would be invulnerable to any attack.

At three o'clock in the afternoon on 6 October 1780, the pursuing rebels managed to surround his position and attacked up the mountainside through the woods from all directions. The plateau on which Ferguson had deployed his troops proved to be too large to defend effectively and the loyalist militia were forced to mount repeated bayonet charges in order to prevent the rebels from gaining a foothold on the high ground. Coming under deadly fire from the rebels, who were concealed amongst the rocks and trees, the loyalists suffered extremely high casualties during these charges. A rebel commander, Colonel Williams, was killed but Ferguson was also mortally wounded while trying to rally his troops. After only half an hour of extremely fierce fighting the entire plateau had been overrun by the rebels. Fired by revenge for the massacre at Waxhaw, the rebels shouted, 'Give 'em Tarleton's Quarter!' One thousand loyalists were killed and captured at a cost of only 28 rebel soldiers. It had been a bitter battle fought between American rebels and American loyalists, and news of this British defeat caused loyalist support to evaporate even further in the Carolinas.

Cornwallis now found himself in increasingly hostile country and with his numbers sharply reduced. He therefore retreated with his exhausted troops south to Winnsborough, where he abandoned all further plans to invade North

Carolina. He decided to limit his operations to maintaining control of South Carolina until he was able to replenish his supplies and reinforce his army. It was while he was resting at Winnsborough that Cornwallis first learned of Clinton's plan to establish a permanent British base in Chesapeake Bay.

By the end of the autumn of 1780, Clinton had lost all interest in launching an attack against the French base on Rhode Island. Even Admiral Rodney, who had that summer sailed across the Atlantic in order to breathe new life into the failing British war effort in North America, could not get Clinton to agree that his immediate priority should be the capture of Rhode Island. He had even offered at one point to command the naval element of the operation himself, but to no avail.

Instead, Clinton had persuaded Rodney that it would be better to take advantage of the secret defection of the American general in West Point, Benedict Arnold, who had promised to betray the garrison to the British in return for £10,000. Arnold had become disillusioned with the revolution because of the way that he had been treated by Congress, which he believed had not sufficiently recognized his personal contribution to the victory at Saratoga. There were also accusations being made against him concerning financial irregularities. Possession of West Point would give the British command of the Highlands, allow them to separate New England from the rest of the rebellious colonies, and complete the northern plan that had been abandoned after the loss of Burgoyne's army at Saratoga. Rodney was unable to disagree with the logic of this argument.

Clinton therefore sent his friend and confidant Major André with a message to Arnold accepting Arnold's proposition. However, André was captured en route and hanged as a spy by Washington. Arnold was therefore forced to flee from West Point and go over to the British side. By then it was too late in the year to revive the plan to attack Rhode Island and Rodney, fearing the onset of winter storms, left for the West Indies and England in October 1780, carrying with him many of Arbuthnot's stores and 400 of his sailors.

The French garrison at Rhode Island meanwhile remained unmolested by the British. 'I would be happy', commented Germain somewhat mildly, 'if our generals had more activity.' It was clear, however, that Clinton urgently needed to take some sort of offensive action against the rebels if he was not to lose the war entirely. His inability to deal with the French garrison in Rhode Island and the collapse of his plan to retake the Highlands in the north therefore forced him once again to look further south. Rather than support Cornwallis directly, he decided to open up a central front against the rebels. If the British could establish a permanent base in Chesapeake Bay, they would be able to attack rebel positions in North Virginia or Maryland and so cut Washington's lines of communication with his army in the south. Ultimately, a British force in Chesapeake Bay would be able to take the pressure off Cornwallis by driving into Virginia from the east. Virginia was Washington's home state and along with Maryland remained an important centre of rebellion.

Therefore on 16 October 1780, quite ignoring the considerable risk of interception by the French fleet, he despatched naval transports to Chesapeake Bay with 2,500 men under command of General Alexander Leslie. His orders were to establish a base on the Elizabeth River, carry out raids on rebel positions at Portsmouth and Richmond, and also make contact with Cornwallis. However, with Cornwallis now back in South Carolina, it was not made clear to Leslie what he should do. In the end, and feeling too inferior in numbers to launch any attacks against the rebels, Leslie headed south to join forces with Cornwallis at Cape Fear in North Carolina. Clinton's attempt to open a second front had failed without a shot being fired.

Germain was furious when he heard the news that his plan to establish a base in Chesapeake Bay had been abandoned. Not only had time and scarce resources been wasted on the attempt, but Chesapeake Bay had again become available as a shipping lane to resupply the French and American Army. Remonstrating with Clinton, he advised him that 'the war should be conducted upon a permanent and settled plan of conquest, always securing and preserving what has been recovered, and not by desultory enterprises taking possession of places at one time, and abandoning them at another, which never can bring the war to a conclusion, or encourage the people to avow their loyalty'. This was wise counsel, but without additional resources from England it would be impossible for Clinton to follow Germain's advice.

In an attempt to rectify matters, Clinton despatched Benedict Arnold to Chesapeake Bay to carry out the assignments that Leslie had failed to undertake. He was instructed to establish a presence there and start attacking the rebel bases in Maryland and Virginia. Arnold chose Leslie's old temporary position at Portsmouth as the location for his new base. From here he could mount attacks against the rebels and also be resupplied by sea. However, the success of the operation depended entirely on Arbuthnot's willingness to support the operation. Arbuthnot, though he was failing in health and blind in one eye, surprisingly rose to the challenge. When the French fleet, encouraged by Washington, set sail from Rhode Island to cut off Arnold from the sea, Arbuthnot sailed out from New York and engaged it. After an indecisive sea battle the French withdrew, and Arbuthnot returned triumphant to New York to receive grudging praise from Clinton.

However, by now it was clear to both Arnold and Clinton that the isolated British base at Portsmouth was too exposed to survive even a minor rebel attack, so Clinton gave orders for the garrison there to be reinforced by 2,000 men. He also replaced Arnold who, although highly successful in carrying out his mission, was not fully trusted by his subordinate officers. He chose his old friend General William Phillips to be his replacement. The British were subsequently able to maintain a permanent base in Chesapeake Bay until the fall of Yorktown, and the actions of both Arnold and Phillips proved both tactically and strategically important. They were able to destroy rebel stores and prevent recruiting by the rebels, and Tarleton's raid on Charlottesville also forced the state government of Virginia to flee across the Blue Ridge Mountains. This led to the disgrace of Thomas Jefferson and his replacement by Patrick Henry. As a Virginian, Washington became extremely worried about the situation in his home state and this influenced his decision to fight the British in Chesapeake Bay rather than in New York, where he had originally planned to attack.

Notwithstanding these local successes, it should have been evident that, on a wider plane, the entire British strategy in North America was failing. Clinton had still not yet brought Washington or his Continental Army to decisive battle. The French had been allowed to maintain a base in Rhode Island, Cornwallis had not succeeded in gaining control of the southern colonies and, most significantly, the French Navy was now able to achieve superiority over the British on the American seaboard – albeit temporarily. At a command level, Clinton had quarrelled not only with Arbuthnot but also with Cornwallis, who had started to follow an agenda set between himself and Germain, rather than with his commander-in-chief. The entire situation was beginning to look like a repeat of the disastrous campaign of 1777 when Clinton had lost contact with both Howe in Philadelphia and Burgoyne in Canada. Certainly, in London, after five years of war Lord North's administration had begun to lose touch with reality.

Chapter Six

In wars of rebellion, there is other knowledge required . . . not only the knowledge of the country,
but the disposition of the people.

GEORGE WASHINGTON

Washington had not had an easy year in 1780. In August of
that year he had had to face up to the consequences of
the desertion of one of his best generals, Benedict Arnold,
and this disaster was soon followed by the defeat of Gates at
Camden and the loss of South Carolina to Cornwallis. At
the same time, the Continental Army remained weakened
by a continual lack of money, supplies and shortage of
recruits. It was still in competition for recruits with the
colonial militias, who were able to offer their soldiers not
only limited engagements, but also far higher wages.
Furthermore, when men served in the militia they were
never deployed far from their homes. Even for the most
ardent revolutionary, this proved to be a more attractive
way of supporting the revolution than by joining Washington's army, which for the past year had in any case done
little in the way of fighting.

It was becoming apparent to Washington that the Congress was in danger of losing the ability to effectively
support the war. Without a new injection of money and
men, it was likely that the Continental Army would have to

disperse. If this happened then the French would abandon their support of the American Revolution and thereafter make peace as best they could with England. By his urgent appeals for a massive resupply of money, men and materials, Washington's emissary in Versailles, Colonel Laurens, had inevitably revealed to the French the dire state of the Continental Army and this had almost persuaded them that the revolution had become a lost cause.

Although the defeat of General Gates at Camden on 18 August 1780 and the rout of the entire American Army in the south by Cornwallis had been a major strategic blow to Washington, there proved to be a silver lining to this particular cloud. For on Washington's advice, Gates was replaced by Nathanael Greene, who had recently been quartermaster general to the Continental Army. Greene was a brilliant conventional tactician who also understood the art of mobile insurgency war. He realized that Cornwallis with his limited resources would not be able to maintain a regular or sufficient military presence in an area as extensive as the Carolinas, in which movement was extremely difficult. Cornwallis would have to disperse his limited manpower, would not be able to rely on the support of the loyalists and could therefore be engaged piecemeal.

Greene's concept of operations was continually to harass and attack Cornwallis's lines of communication using the rebel militias, while he drew Cornwallis deep into the back country and away from the coast where the British support bases lay. Mobility would be the key to his own success, and as the country over which he would fight was bisected by many rivers, he ordered flat-bottom boats to be built that he could also take with him when he marched over land. This would allow him to cross rivers at points of his choosing, rather than having to rely on the few fording places as the British had to do. In support of his mobile strategy, he asked Washington for cavalry and light infantry. In response to this request, Washington sent Colonel Henry Lee's mixed cavalry and mounted infantry unit to support him. Henceforth, Greene would be able to reinforce these regular units with the militias and by so concentrating his forces he hoped to annihilate the numerically weaker enemy.

Greene arrived to take command of the southern army in December 1780 and found waiting for him a dispirited, ill-disciplined, irregular mix of militia and partisans, on whom he could not readily depend. 'The wants of this army are so numerous and various that the shortest way of telling you is to inform you that we have nothing,' he wrote in one of his reports to Congress. Nevertheless, he was determined to put his concept of operations into practice straight away. The soldiers would have to learn their military skills the hard way – in battle. In January 1781, he divided his forces into two elements, sending Morgan with some 600 Continental soldiers supported by militia across the Catawba River to threaten the British posts at Augusta and the British post at Ninety Six. Meanwhile, he would threaten Cornwallis directly from his base at Cheraw on the Pee Dee River. Writing to Washington, he explained that this plan 'makes most of my inferior force for it compels my adversary to divide his, and holds him in doubt as to his own line of conduct. He cannot leave Morgan behind him to come to me, or his posts of Ninety Six and Augusta would be exposed. And he cannot chase Morgan far, or prosecute his views upon Virginia whilst I am here with the whole country before me.' He added that he 'would only turn upon his adversary and fight him when he pleased'. This plan was a classic example of insurgency warfare and would be repeated many times in the future, not least by Wellington in the Peninsular War, Mao Tse-tung during the

Long March, General Giap in Vietnam and most recently by the insurgents in Iraq.

Cornwallis was compelled to react to Greene's new initiative. Sending Tarleton to intercept and destroy Morgan's rebel force, on 7 January 1781 he himself set off with a force of 4,000 men to establish a blocking line in order to prevent Greene from reinforcing Morgan. He also wanted to bring Greene to battle. Unfortunately for the British, Morgan had no need of reinforcements from Greene as the veteran of so many battles was quite capable of looking after himself.

On learning of Tarleton's approach, Morgan had deployed his small force on grazing grounds between two rivers called Cowpens, thus making escape impossible for his more inexperienced militia if they came under undue pressure. He then laid out his main defensive position in three separate lines of battle. In the front were Morgan's sharpshooters – the same men who had done such damage at Saratoga. Behind them came the militia, and to the rear on a hill were the regular soldiers of the Continental Army. Morgan ignored his exposed flanks, as they lay between a ravine and a river. The sharpshooters were ordered to fire two volleys at the enemy, but only 'at killing distance', and then fall back. The militia were also ordered to fire two shots and then retreat to a location behind the main defensive position on the hill. Their retreat, it was hoped, would cause the British to rush forward and expose themselves to the fire of the main force from its position on the high ground. Morgan believed that the British would already have suffered considerable casualties by the time they arrived at his main position. As he explained to his men, 'The whole idea is to lead Benny [Tarleton] into a trap so we can beat his cavalry and infantry as they come up those slopes. When they've been cut down to size by our fire, we'll attack them.'

His plan worked perfectly, for Tarleton had completely misread the tactical situation, believing that victory would be easily won because Morgan was apparently trapped between two rivers. He assumed that the inexperienced rebel soldiers would not be able to withstand a frontal assault by regular British troops. Accordingly, Tarleton drove straight into the trap.

After opening fire and killing a number of Tarleton's advance guard, the sharpshooters duly retreated. The militiamen then fired two volleys, as instructed, and also withdrew. By the time that Tarleton's men had reached the main rebel defensive position they had suffered a large number of casualties, nearly half of whom were officers, from the deadly fire of the sharpshooters and militiamen. Nevertheless, the British continued to attack, only to come under even more intense fire from the soldiers of the Continental Army. Surprised that the Americans were not by now fleeing from the advancing British, Tarleton committed his reserve. At this point the Americans counterattacked as planned, with their infantry in the centre and cavalry on the British flanks. Caught so completely in Morgan's deadly trap, the British had no option but to surrender. Tarleton himself made good his escape, but only after shooting the horse of a Colonel Washington who was pursuing him. The British had lost 340 men killed and 525 captured. The Americans had lost 12 killed and 61 wounded. It had been a massive defeat for the British, who could ill afford to lose such numbers.

Cornwallis, infuriated by the defeat of Tarleton, now became even more determined to bring Greene to battle. In spite of Tarleton's defeat, he still believed that he could destroy Nathanael Greene's Continental Army. If he accomplished this, then the rebel militias in the south would be powerless to prevent the British forces from taking control of the entire Carolinas. Without telling Clinton of his plans, Cornwallis decided to march north in the hope of catching Greene. Nothing could have better played into the hands of Greene, who immediately realized that any move into North Carolina would seriously overstretch the British. Staying faithful to the old insurgent adage that 'when the enemy advances, you retire; when the enemy retires, you advance', Greene retreated before Cornwallis – but not before giving orders to the rebel militias to mount continuous attacks against the British flanks and supply lines.

As Greene slipped away north across the flooded winter rivers of the Carolinas, Cornwallis gave pursuit. Knowing that he would never catch up with Greene while he was encumbered by his heavy transports, he gave orders to abandon them. His deputy commander, O'Hara, reported back to England: 'Without baggage, necessaries or provisions of any sort for officer or soldier, in the most barren inhospitable unhealthy part of North America, opposed to the most savage inveterate perfidious cruel enemy, with zeal and bayonets it was resolved to follow Greene's army to the end of the world.'

These were bold intentions that were to be sorely put to the test over the next few weeks as Greene drew Cornwallis ever deeper into North Carolina. Marching up to 30 miles a day across flooded countryside and swollen rivers, Cornwallis finally pushed Greene across the Dan River into Virginia. The pursuit, known as the 'Race to the Dan', had lasted three months, during which time Cornwallis had covered over 200 miles. But his army had become wholly exhausted and was also desperately short of supplies. It was now the turn of Cornwallis to retreat. The hunter had become the hunted. Finally, Greene caught up with Cornwallis at the Guilford Court House in North Carolina on 15 March 1781, where he forced Cornwallis to stand and fight.

Like Morgan at Cowpens, Greene had laid out his defences in three lines. The North Carolina and Virginia militia formed the first two lines, with soldiers of the Continental Army making up the last line. However, the lines were well separated and could not provide each other with mutually supporting fire.

After subjecting the Americans to artillery fire for nearly half an hour, Cornwallis gave orders for the attack to commence at half past one in the afternoon. As at Cowpens, the British troops fought their way through the first two lines, which gave way, but once again they suffered high casualties. By the time that they arrived at Greene's main position, the British troops had become disorientated in the thickly wooded country and failed to concentrate their attack. While the British and American soldiers were engaged in fierce but confused hand-to-hand fighting, Cornwallis ordered his artillery to fire grapeshot directly into the fighting masses of Americans and British. This resulted in many casualties on both sides, but caused the American rebels to break off the engagement. Technically, the battle had been won by Cornwallis, but he was never able to recover from the high cost of 600 British troops killed. Charles James Fox, an English Whig opposed to the war, on hearing news of the battle commented laconically, 'Another such victory will ruin the British Army.'

Cornwallis, who again realized that his army could not sustain the high tempo of combat, decided to withdraw, this time to Wilmington on the coast. Had the war in the south been waged by Greene as a conventional war, Cornwallis would in all probability have won. He had, after all, never lost a battle to Greene. But this was no conventional war. It was a guerrilla war where the insurgents could accept defeat as long as they were able to stay in existence and also retain the support of the population. As long as these basic elements were in place, they would always be able to inflict casualties on the enemy. As Clinton wrote after the battle, 'we may conquer but we shall never keep'.

Not at all discouraged by his failure to annihilate the British army at Guilford Court House, Greene resumed his guerrilla tactics. He started attacking isolated British posts and ambushing any small British detachments that were still operating in the south. Writing to Washington after the battle, Greene explained his guerrilla tactics: 'We fight, we get beat, we fight again.'

Such had been his success in wearing down Cornwallis's army that, for a second time, Cornwallis gave up his hope of ever defeating the American insurgency in North Carolina, which was regarded by Germain as 'the road to Virginia'. Without telling Clinton, he decided to join forces with Phillips and Arnold in Chesapeake Bay, from where he hoped that the combined British forces would finally be able to launch an invasion into the southern colonies. He left Wilmington on 25 April 1781 and arrived a month later in Chesapeake 200 miles away having been entirely unopposed by the rebels en route.

The same day that Cornwallis departed for Chesapeake Bay, Nathanael Greene began to threaten the British post at Camden with a force of 1,200 men. He hoped to overrun the well-protected fort, which was commanded by Lieutenant Colonel Lord Francis Rawdon. However, it became clear to Greene that he could not attack the post without heavy artillery. Since he had only three light cannon, he decided to establish a defensive position astride a road 2 miles from Camden at a place called Hobkirk's Hill. Even though the British were considerably outnumbered by the rebels, Rawdon with 800 men marched out of his secure base and engaged Greene's troops in a wide-flanking movement to the American left. A fierce battle ensued in which

Rawdon used snipers to pick off American officers. This caused the rebels to retreat and the British finally won the day. But, once again, their losses were unacceptable both militarily and politically. The British people were becoming tired of the war in America. It had also been a worthless action from a tactical point of view, as Rawdon was forced to abandon the post some days later because of a shortage of troops and a lack of supplies. Subsequently, all the British and loyalist posts in the back country of the Carolinas were captured by the rebels, who often treated the defenders with great savagery. By the middle of September, the entire Carolinas had fallen into the hands of the rebels. Greene had lost every battle that he fought against the British except one, but nevertheless he had prevented the British from succeeding in their campaign to pacify the southern colonies. It was a classic example of insurgency warfare.

None of this was yet apparent to Washington, who had spent the winter of 1780 quartered with his Continental Army near Morristown in Pennsylvania. Indeed, the situation seemed to him to be increasingly hopeless, given the lack of material support that Congress was able to give him and his troops. At Christmas, General Wayne had described the soldiers' condition as being 'Poorly clothed, badly fed, and worse paid, some of them have not received a paper dollar for near twelve months.' On 1 January 1781, a mutiny broke out in the army, and a group of mutineers marched on Philadelphia. President of Congress Joseph Reed determined to meet them and rode to their camp near Princeton. Happily for him, he discovered that the mutineers had already refused a request from the British that they should desert; in fact, they avowed that should the British launch an attack into Pennsylvania, they would return to Reed's command. Reed agreed with the mutineers that a commission be set up to look into their demands, particularly those relating to their terms of engagement and pay. The result of these negotiations was such that the mutineers, whose loyalty to the cause was never in question, peacefully returned to their original command. However, a second mutiny in New Jersey was put down with more force and two of the mutineers were hanged.

In March 1781, Washington had again written in some desperation to Laurens in Paris: 'Without a foreign loan our present force, which is but the remnant of an army, cannot be kept together this campaign, much less will it be increased and in readiness for another . . . you may rely on it as a fact that we cannot transport the provisions from the States in which they are assessed as we cannot pay the teamsters . . . in a word we are at the end of our tether . . . now or never our deliverance must come.' In the meantime, one of his generals, Lafayette, was forced to borrow money from the merchants of Baltimore to pay for his troops' military equipment. It was only then that he could afford to move to Virginia and carry out his orders from Washington to prevent the British making raids on rebel bases in the Chesapeake area.

The news that 3,000 Hessians had arrived from Europe to reinforce Clinton in New York further depressed Washington. He explained to the governors of the eastern states that all his future plans depended 'upon the degree of vigor with which the executives of the States exercise the powers passed for filling up and supplying the army'. Without men and material, the revolution could not be continued. Fortunately, the French were about to come to his rescue.

For Vergennes, the French foreign minister at Versailles, had finally persuaded Louis XVI to make one last attempt to break the British hold on the North American colonies. As a result, on 22 March 1781 Admiral de Grasse had sailed from Brest for the West Indies on his flagship, *Ville de Paris*, which was the pride of the French Navy. In reply, the British sent only three ships of the line, thus again ceding naval superiority to the French. In May, Washington attended a conference at Wethersfield in Connecticut in the house of Joseph Webb. His son, Sidney Webb, had been aide-de-camp to Washington at the battles of Trenton and Princeton and was therefore highly trusted. The meeting had been called by Rochambeau, the land commander of French forces in North America. At this conference, Washington was informed that de Grasse would sail north to break the blockade of Rhode Island. Following this, the combined American and French forces would attack either Clinton in New York or Cornwallis in Chesapeake. It was finally decided that their objective would be Cornwallis's army in Chesapeake, which directly threatened Washington's home state, Virginia.

Meanwhile, Clinton had passed yet another leisurely summer of almost complete inactivity in New York, still believing that he could win the war in America. He had been greatly encouraged by the news of the mutiny in Washington's army during the previous winter and although the British had been forced to withdraw from the Carolinas by the guerrilla campaign of Nathanael Greene, Cornwallis still posed a considerable threat to the south from his new base in Chesapeake Bay. Furthermore, the British Army remained in firm control of New York and the French were still bottled up in Rhode Island. There was also a good chance that the French might not continue to support the American Revolution, given the costly war with England that this had caused and the lack of success experienced by their expeditionary forces in North America. Clinton expected naval reinforcements to arrive from England that summer, which he hoped would give him clear naval superiority, even if the French also reinforced their fleet. All Clinton felt that he needed to do was to avoid defeat and the war would surely be won.

Back in England, Germain had become exceedingly worried about Clinton's lack of concern for the safety of Cornwallis's isolated army in Chesapeake, which would clearly be put at risk by the arrival of any further French naval reinforcements in North America. Finally, he prevailed on Clinton to take action, and on 20 July 1781 Cornwallis received orders from Clinton telling him to develop and fortify a permanent base somewhere of his choosing in Chesapeake. The orders were typically vague and gave no indication as to where the base should be. Given such latitude, Cornwallis, who had spent the past month fruitlessly trying to pin down Lafayette in north Virginia, decided to divide his forces and establish them in two separate positions on opposite sides of the York River at Yorktown and Gloucester. This was a questionable decision as he had insufficient forces to defend both locations properly and his ships were unable to manoeuvre in the narrow straits that separated the two positions. To make matters worse, at the beginning of August, Admiral Rodney sailed for England. Although in poor health, he was probably still the only naval commander capable of defeating de Grasse. He relinquished command of the West Indies fleet to the unimpressive Admiral Graves, who was to falter at a critical moment in British naval history.

Meanwhile, Washington, who saw that the arrival of de Grasse had radically altered the strategic balance in his favour, determined to attack where the British were at their weakest – in Chesapeake. The French army under Rochambeau joined forces with Washington in early July and together they moved south, leaving only 2,000 troops of the Continental Army behind to guard the Highlands.

But even now Clinton did nothing but sulk and vaguely play with the idea of mounting diversionary attacks into Philadelphia or against Rhode Island to the north. His indecision and extraordinary failure to prevent the allied move south or to reinforce Cornwallis in Chesapeake has confirmed many historians' view that while Clinton may have had a good grasp of tactics, he was hopeless at dealing with large-scale questions of strategy and entirely failed to understand the requirements of higher command.

By mid August, as Cornwallis's troops were starting to dig fortifications in the sandy soil on the banks of the York River, de Grasse was sailing from the West Indies with twenty-eight ships of the line and 3,000 men. They had not been intercepted en route by the British Navy and so he was able to detach four ships to escort the troops up the James River to join forces with Washington. Meanwhile, Cornwallis, who had little confidence that his defensive work would be able to withstand an attack by the combined French and American forces, wrote to Clinton that to prepare effective defences would be 'work of great time and labour, and after all, I fear will not be very strong'. He was, nevertheless, able to convince himself that Clinton and the British Navy would be able to come to his help long before his positions were threatened or overrun.

His hopes were not to be fulfilled. On 5 September 1781, the British and French fleets met off Chesapeake Bay in what has been called 'one of the least inspiring and most indecisive battles of the century'. De Grasse, who had twenty-four ships, not only outnumbered the British fleet of nineteen ships, but also outgunned them, for he had 1,800 guns against 1,400. In addition, Admiral Graves lacked the offensive spirit of Rodney or Nelson, and although the British initially had the advantage of being upwind, Graves failed to close with the French fleet.

Importantly, he allowed Barras, who had sailed from Rhode Island with the all-important French artillery siege train, to slip into Chesapeake Bay. After some discussion with his second-in-command, Admiral Hood, who strongly urged re-engagement with the French, Graves decided, nonetheless, to break contact and sail back to New York. Although the sea battle had been a tactical draw in terms of losses suffered, its strategic impact was quite disastrous for the British. The French were now in control of Chesapeake Bay and Cornwallis's position had become untenable. To save his fleet, Graves had sacrificed Cornwallis and the American colonies. But, by so doing, he may well have saved the West Indies and Canada for the British Empire.

On 14 September 1781, Washington and Rochambeau arrived in Williamsburg, some 14 miles from Yorktown, where they joined forces with Lafayette. On hearing news of their approach, Cornwallis accelerated his defensive work, which consisted of two main entrenchments around York-town that were protected by a number of redoubts. He had also moored his own three ships stem to stern in a half-circle on the river in front of Yorktown. He had removed their land-side guns and turned their sails into tents: there was going to be no retreat by sea. His forces were out-numbered two to one. On 28 September 1781, Washington and Rochambeau marched on Yorktown and after a desultory exchange of fire from outlying British picquets they settled their armies down for a siege.

In New York, Clinton had finally reacted to the desperate situation of Cornwallis and his small army at Yorktown and was preparing to reinforce him by sea, observing that ''Tis not a move of choice but of necessity. If Lord Cornwallis's army falls, I should have little hope of seeing British dominion re-established in America.' On 29 September, Cornwallis received the welcome news from Clinton that a

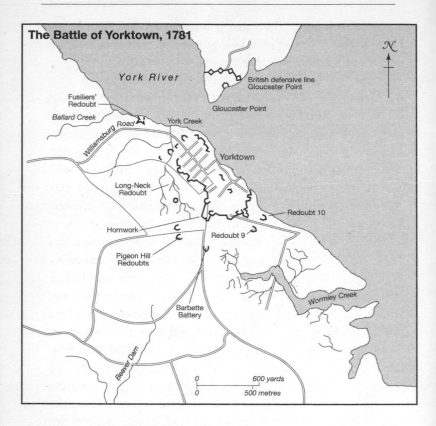

The Battle of Yorktown, 1781

York River

British defensive line
Gloucester Point

Fusiliers'
Redoubt

Ballard Creek

Gloucester Point

Williamsburg Road

York Creek

Yorktown

Long-Neck
Redoubt

Redoubt 10

Hornwork

Redoubt 9

Pigeon Hill
Redoubts

Wormley Creek

Barbette
Battery

Beaver Dam

| 0 | 600 yards |
| 0 | 500 metres |

British fleet of twenty-three ships of the line and 5,000
soldiers would leave New York on 5 October for Chesapeake. Even allowing for time spent in passage, Cornwallis
believed that it would still be possible to hold on at Yorktown until these reinforcements arrived. However, in spite
of the fact that time was fast running out for Cornwallis,
Admiral Graves was not prepared to set sail until his fleet
had been reinforced by further ships expected from England
and the ships damaged in the battle on 5 September 1781
had been fully repaired. Even though his fleet had already
been reinforced by the arrival of three ships under

command of Admiral Digby, it was not until 19 October – the day that Cornwallis finally surrendered to Washington – that the fleet finally sailed.

In the words of one of the besiegers, Cornwallis was 'in a bottle and the cork was about to be driven in'. It was the French and American artillery that was finally to drive that cork in, for Cornwallis had no reply to the continuous bombardment of his positions, at a time when his own artillery was fast running out of shells and his army was short of supplies. On 29 September 1781 – the same day that he had received news of Clinton's rescue plan – Cornwallis unexpectedly withdrew from his outer defences in order to shorten his line of defence. This decision allowed the French and American artillery to advance unchallenged to new positions from where it could direct observed fire against the entire British defensive line at Yorktown. Nowhere was safe, and Cornwallis was forced to place his headquarters in an underground bunker. His situation rapidly worsened after the capture of two major redoubts, 9A and 10, by the French and American forces on 14 October 1781. A slight quarrel had occurred amongst the allies when Lafayette gave command of the assault on Redoubt 10 to one of his most trusted staff officers, Colonel de Gimat. However, Lieutenant Colonel Alexander Hamilton, who had spent most of the war as secretary to Washington and was taking part in the assault with his New York and Connecticut battalion, was determined not to miss an opportunity for a senior command. He therefore appealed personally to Washington, who countermanded Lafayette's orders and gave Hamilton his moment of glory. Hamilton, leading his men bravely if somewhat foolhardily, successfully captured the redoubt after fierce hand-to-hand fighting. Hamilton later went on to become the first Secretary of the Treasury. After losing the two redoubts,

Cornwallis wrote to Clinton, stating that 'my situation now becomes very critical . . . the safety of the place is therefore so precarious that I cannot recommend that the fleet and army should run great risk in endeavouring to save us'. It was perfectly clear from this message that by then Cornwallis had given up all hope. He knew full well that without reinforcements his positions would shortly be overrun by the Americans and French.

In a somewhat futile gesture, Cornwallis and Tarleton discussed a surprise breakout to try and save Cornwallis's army. Had there not been a sudden squall on the night of 16 October, Cornwallis might well have got his men across the York River and attempted a breakout. However, Washington had anticipated such a move. He had ordered all the skiffs and flatboats on the York River above Yorktown to be moved to a place just upstream from his army so that, if necessary, he could cross his force rapidly and reinforce the allies in Gloucester. Furthermore, the French and Americans now had all the cavalry, for Tarleton and other British commanders had been destroying their horses for lack of feed. Even had the weather cooperated with Cornwallis and allowed him to evacuate Yorktown, there was little chance that his exhausted and depleted army could have escaped from Washington and rejoined Clinton in New York.

Therefore, on 17 October 1781 Cornwallis finally sent an officer, accompanied by a drummer, under a white flag of truce across to the Americans to discuss terms for surrender. These being agreed, the next day the British Army marched out of their positions and laid down their weapons as their band played a song called 'The World Turned Upside Down'. The official surrender, which took place on 19 October 1781, was not attended by Cornwallis, who pleaded ill health.

It has been frequently argued that had Cornwallis not

given up his outer defensive line so early on, and thus rendered his inner defences unsustainable, it is likely that the British could have held out for sufficient time for Clinton to arrive with reinforcements. A decisive blow against Washington at this point would almost certainly have persuaded the French to withdraw their support to the Americans. However, this reasoning depends on the vital assumption that Graves could have defeated a superior French fleet that was still guarding the approaches to Chesapeake. Whatever may have been the causes of the loss of Cornwallis's entire army at Yorktown, the inadequacy of the British Navy and the cautious nature of Graves finally brought to an end British hope of ever defeating the rebellious Americans. Nevertheless, it was still not clear at that time either to Washington or to the French that the war was effectively over, for as Vergennes said on hearing the news of the surrender of Cornwallis's army at Yorktown, 'History offers few examples of a success so complete: but one would be wrong to believe that it means an immediate peace. It is not in the English character to give up so easily.'

Operationally, the British still had an army in North America whose strength amounted to over 30,000 men. They had formidable garrisons in Canada, New York, Charleston, Savannah and St Augustine. De Grasse would soon be forced to return to the West Indies with his fleet in order to avoid the winter storms and Washington's army was still as poorly maintained by Congress as ever, although de Grasse had bought supplies from the French to improve its situation.

At a strategic level, however, it was clear that to continue the war in North America would be to risk losing Britain's position as a global power, for everywhere its interests were now being threatened by nations that only a few years earlier had been comprehensively defeated in successive wars. By the autumn of 1781, the French were simultaneously preparing to send expeditionary forces to the West Indies and India in order to wrest control of these important trading regions from the British. The Spanish had already taken West Florida, Tobago had been lost, and a combined French and Spanish attack on Jamaica was now imminent. In the Mediterranean, the French were about to capture Minorca, and the Spanish and French fleets once again threatened the Channel approaches. At home, the financial cost of the war had been enormous. The British people had lost faith in their politicians. The only sensible solution was to now sue for peace in America.

Nevertheless, it was to be another year before a peace treaty was signed bringing the American War of Independence to an end, during which time only a few minor skirmishes took place in the south. This long delay was caused by the continuing refusal of George III and Germain to accept the inevitability of American independence. This unrealistic and absurd stance was not effectively challenged in Parliament by the Whig opposition, who still felt that it would be unpatriotic to argue the case for American independence. However, on 22 February 1782 Parliament finally voted to end the 'coercion of America', and a month later the North Ministry resigned, making way for Rockingham, who had always opposed the war.

The same year, on 10 April, Rodney defeated de Grasse's fleet at Iles des Saintes in the West Indies, thereby persuading the French to agree a peace treaty with Britain. Accordingly, on 3 September 1783 separate treaties were signed in Paris between Britain and America and between Britain, France, Spain and the Netherlands. A civil war that had begun with militant rebels firing a few shots at the British in Lexington and ended in global conflict was finally over.

No more important example exists in history of a small group of determined insurgents defeating a world superpower than that of the British defeat in the American War of Independence. Subsequently, there have been many other successful examples of liberation movements in history – most notably the one led by Mao Tse-tung. But the consequences of the liberation of the thirteen colonies in North America from British rule were arguably far more significant in terms of shaping world history than the establishment of Communism in China. For it allowed freedom and democracy to become rooted in significant parts of the New World, an event that subsequently enabled these two fundamental principles to be preserved in Europe by America in the twentieth century when they were in such danger of being extinguished during two world wars and subsequently during the Cold War. Although the legacy of American independence has created a political force for good in the world today, the strategic lessons of the American War of Independence seem to have been largely forgotten, not least by the Americans themselves in Vietnam and Iraq.

Conclusion

War is the parent of illusions.   H. A. L. FISHER

The illusion that even the most powerful military power in the world could defeat an insurgency at long distance, against a determined people who had an entirely different set of values from its own, cost Britain its thirteen American colonies, eight West Indies islands, Minorca and Florida, and almost lost India. It caused a belief amongst the rulers of Europe that Britain had passed its zenith and, like the Roman Empire before it, was now in a state of unstoppable decline. It had taken just eighteen years from the Peace of Paris in 1763, which had established Britain as the pre-eminent power of the age, to the battle of Yorktown. The brash pioneering spirit of the New World had revealed the corruptions and deficiencies of the Old.

When Cornwallis's defeated army marched out of Yorktown in 1781, George III and his ministers were convinced that the withdrawal of British troops from the thirteen colonies and the acceptance of defeat that it entailed, would result not only in anarchy in America but the collapse of the entire British Empire. France and Spain would seize our remaining colonies in America, the West Indies, the Mediterranean and also in India. Worse still, the Irish, heartened by the success of the American rebellion, would rise up against the British. By the end of the century, Great Britain would have become no more than an unimportant island off the northwest coast of Europe.

But of course, George III's strategic assessment of the consequences of the defeat at Yorktown – like everything else that he had been responsible for during the War of Independence – was entirely wrong. For it was by finally accepting defeat in what at that time was a relatively unimportant part of the world that Great Britain was able to focus on what really mattered: continuing to build its influence and empire across the globe. If the opposition led by Rockingham, Fox and Pitt had not had the moral courage and vision to accept defeat against the American colonists or had not been able to persuade the King and his ministers to do likewise, Britain would have indeed lost its position in the world, and today the people of the largest democracy in the world, India, would either be speaking French or Portuguese.

During the eight bloody and cruel years of the war, George III had followed a hopelessly flawed strategy in dealing with the American rebellion and he had also throughout that time failed to commit adequate resources to the mission. He had never understood the character or nature of the American people, and he had greatly underestimated their determination to throw off the yoke of British rule. The War of Independence had never just been about 'taxation without representation'. It had been about the freedom for Americans to develop their own society in the way that they wished. They firmly believed in the principles of good governance that derived from the political theories of John Locke. Indeed, the *Boston Gazette* in 1773 had published a popular edition of Locke's *Second Treatise* in order 'to give every intelligent reader a better view of the Rights of Men'. It was not merely the intellectual elite of New England but ordinary American people who came to understand that the logical consequences of Locke's political theory entailed complete independence from British rule.

On the other side of the Atlantic a similar view had been formed by the Whigs. Although Lord North, the British Prime Minister and architect of the war, on hearing the news of the defeat at Yorktown, threw his arms in the air and exclaimed, 'Oh, God, it's all over', in fact the end of the war signalled the re-emergence of Britain as a global power, and the start of the building of a new nation. In 1783, Britain was on the threshold of the industrial revolution and a young genius, William Pitt had become Prime Minister of Britain. He was able to see beyond the end of the war with America and begin the process of Britain's political and economic recovery. He could also see that war with France was looming, and no time could be wasted in terms of re-establishing Britain's naval supremacy. Under the energetic direction of the Duke of York, the new commander in chief appointed in 1795, the military efficiency and administration of the British army was greatly improved. Within thirty-five years, Britain, along with its allies Russia, Prussia and Austria was able to defeat Napoleon and his Grande Armée – the most powerful army the world had ever seen.

These were no easy tasks since Britain was facing near bankruptcy when peace was officially signed with America in Paris two years after Yorktown. Her national debt amounted to £200m as a result of the French Indian War and the American rebellion. At the time annual government revenue totalled no more than £13m, and most of this sum was being spent on interest payments. Pitt however realised that Britain was about to experience unprecedented economic growth made possible by the incipient industrial revolution. By reducing taxation, he not only increased government revenue but in doing so also created the necessary economic conditions for Britain to become the workshop of the world. Trade resumed with America with Britain importing raw materials from America and sending manufactured goods back in return. Within a decade, it was at pre-war levels.

Furthermore, in 1784 Pitt also passed the India Bill, thus ensuring that the poor administration that had so unnecessarily soured relations with the American colonies could not happen elsewhere in the good governance of the British Empire. He also set about removing the corruptions of the British parliamentary system and limited the personal role of the King in policy making. His far sighted parliamentary reforms finally culminated in the abolishment of slavery in 1807 and the Great Reform Act of 1832.

Following Britain's withdrawal from the American colonies, the Royal Navy was brought up to the previous wartime establishment of ninety-three ships of the line. Pitt took a close personal interest in the navy and, as Prime Minister, would often visit the shipyards to ensure that ships were being constructed on time. A modern breed of naval and military commanders were appointed – men like Vincent and Nelson or Wellington and Moore. These were leaders who understood the art of war and inspired their officers and men in battle. In the Iberian peninsula, the British experience of fighting against guerrillas in North America gave confidence to Wellington, who saw that the French Army in Spain would find it equally impossible both to pacify the country and at the same time bring Wellington to decisive battle. In the event he proved correct, for too many of the French troops in Spain had to be committed to counter-insurgency operations. From that time on, the British began to understand how to wage not only just war but also counter-insurgency warfare, for during the next 150 years the British were to be faced with the problem of keeping control of their vast Empire in the face of uprising and mutiny. They became good at small wars, especially counter-insurgency campaigns, something that is particularly relevant to the unconventional wars that are predominantly being fought in the world today.

The American way of war, however, took a different turn. Initially preoccupied in extending its territorial boundaries to the west, after two abortive raids of Canada in 1812, the newly independent America's first full-scale war took place in Mexico in 1846. But it was at home, on American soil, that the US Army learned the bloody art of modern conflict during the terrible four years of the American Civil War. Thereafter, without an overseas empire to maintain, the principal role of the army was to pacify the plains and mountain Indian tribes of the west. In doing so, it became the key agency in the colonization of America. The army was also committed to the defence of America through the military dominance of its neighbours in Latin America – something that it did by conventional military intervention. Even when America became involved in an insurgency war in the Philippines in 1899–1913, it chose to use conventional means to fight the insurgents. The lessons studied at the US Army staff college following the First World War were concerned with how to make use of the new technologies of aircraft and radio communications, rather than how to fight insurgency wars. It was not until the Second World War that the US Army started to seriously study the art of insurgency war. This inevitably became a central part of US military doctrine during the Cold War, when the Communist bloc so effectively used revolutionary warfare against the West, especially in Vietnam.

Nevertheless, the considerable successes won by the US Special Forces units in Latin America during the Cold War and the early stages of the Vietnam War were later eclipsed by the failure of US conventional forces to successfully deal with the Vietcong. The clear lesson that emerged from that war and subsequently the Russian defeat in Afghanistan was that an insurgency cannot be fought successfully by conventional means. This lesson has somehow been forgotten by many Americans, for today there is a widespread belief – not amongst the military, but in the Bush administration – that the brilliance, sophistication and superiority of US military power has given America an invincibility in all forms of war. This belief has now been put to the test in the Middle East, in support of the war against global terrorists.

In his valedictory address to the people of the United States, George Washington observed, 'Sympathy for the favourite nation, facilitating the illusion of an imaginary common interest in cases where no real common interest exists, and infusing into one the enmities of the other, betrays the former into a participation of the quarrels and wars of the latter without adequate inducement or justification . . . the great rule of conduct for us, in regard to our foreign nations, is in extending our commercial relations, to have with them as little political connection as possible.' Yet America has long maintained a close relationship with Israel that has made it impossible for them to act as an impartial broker in the Middle East.

Following the invasion of Iraq, there is a strong suspicion in the minds of many Arabs and other Muslims around the world that the US has now embarked on a policy of attacking the enemies of Israel under cover of the war against terrorism. Such a view, whether false or not, clearly makes it impossible for it to be regarded as an impartial player in the Middle East. George Bush is either ignorant of George Washington's views regarding national alliances or he has chosen to ignore them. Either way, chiefly as a result of the disastrous management of the war in Iraq, Bush's reputation in history as a statesman is likely to be the reverse of that held by his well-regarded predecessor, George Washington. For according to Madeleine Albright, the former US Secretary of State, the war in Iraq has been 'the worst foreign policy disaster' ever to be visited upon the United States of America. Certainly, Washington understood far better than Bush that where foreign policy is concerned, nations should have no friends – only interests.

The dilemma facing any occupying power is always how to leave a country when faced by continuing resistance. In this respect the US objective in Iraq has remained remarkably consistent throughout the turbulent years of the occupation. President Bush has stated that the Americans will withdraw only when they have established good governance based on democratic rule, the civil reconstruction of Iraq has been completed, and the Iraqis have assumed responsibility for their own security. They 'will go when the job is done', according to Bush. However, after four years of struggle and sacrifice by the American people, after hundreds of billions of dollars have been expended, and at a terrible cost in human lives, none of these objectives looked remotely feasible. Corruption had become as great a problem for the good governance of Iraq as the insurgency. Civil reconstruction was at a standstill, partly because much of the earmarked money has been either stolen or spent. The hoped-for inward foreign investment has failed to materialize – which is not surprising, given the lack of security in the country. The armed militias and high level of intersectarian killing had brought the country to the brink of civil war. Finally, after four years of remaining in denial, some acknowledgement was made by George Bush that it is not possible to defeat the insurgency by military force. His remaining hope that the Iraqi government can somehow transform itself into one of national unity and thus end the sectarian slaughter looked slender indeed.

Nevertheless, because the Iraqi people so desperately want an end to the conflict that is taking place in their country, the prospect for peace and stability in Iraq is not entirely without hope. Certainly, it is not inevitable that the country will dissolve into civil war and ultimately fragment into three separate political units. For not only do most Iraqis want their country to remain a unified state based on a federal structure, but their neighbours in Iran, Turkey, Syria and the Gulf States also unequivocally wish to see the same.

Within Iraq, the US-led occupation force has become more of an obstacle than a help towards establishing peace and order. For as long as foreign troops remain on their soil, the Iraqi resistance will continue and there can be no hope of a final peace. Withdrawal is not a question of defeat; it is merely recognition, as the British realized in North America in the eighteenth century, that the original objectives can no longer be achieved. The Revolutionary War was unpopular at home and affected Britain's position in the world so adversely that Britain was in danger of losing its global supremacy. The decision to withdraw was a bitter pill for George III and his war cabinet to swallow. But there was no alternative. In the event, Britain quickly recovered its position, and all fears of anarchy and chaos occurring in its former colonies in North America proved groundless. The colonial rebels, once they had responsibility for their own destiny proved, not surprisingly, to be responsible people.

In the same way, the withdrawal of the US occupation force from Iraq should be seen in the context of the war against global terror. After the battle of Yorktown in 1781, Britain recognized that a position had been reached when to continue with the war was wholly counter-productive to its wider strategic goals. Today America, in Iraq, finds itself in much the same position as Britain in 1781. Distracted and diminished by an irrelevant, costly and probably unwinnable war in Iraq, America could ultimately find itself challenged for global supremacy by countries like China and India. Unless America can find someone with the vision and moral courage of William Pitt to lead them away from the war in Iraq, then there is a strong probability that America will ultimately relinquish its position as a global super power, possibly to a regime that will not pursue those ideals of justice and liberty that America has worked so hard to bring to the peoples of the world. The outcome of a withdrawal from Iraq may not necessarily be the doomsday scenario that those opposing it suggest. The gloomy predictions about what would happen in Vietnam when the Americans withdrew were similarly confounded when the so-called domino theory failed to materialize. No other country in the region became Communist and twenty-five years later, Vietnam has become a strong trading partner of the US and a popular tourist destination for Americans.

To argue, as President Bush has done, that the US pulled its troops out of Vietnam too early, because this allowed genocide to take place in neighbouring Cambodia, is to confuse cause and effect. It was the temporary presence of US troops in Cambodia that toppled the existing government and made way for the Khmer Rouge. The continuing presence of US troops in Vietnam could not have halted the slaughter.

The immediate situation in Iraq, following a complete withdrawal of foreign troops, may indeed be bloody and tumultuous, but it is unlikely to be protracted. The twentieth-century history of Iraq has always been punctuated by violent upheavals, which have invariably ended in a military coup.

In September 2007 Ambassador Crocker and General Petraeus made a report to Congress on the political and security situation in Iraq following the surge in force levels that had taken place earlier in the year. Both men sounded a note of cautious optimism and their report has finally allowed President Bush to move towards the only viable policy option still open to him which is to declare victory and start planning the withdrawal of American troops from Iraq. However, to avoid leaving Iraq in control of an Iranian-influenced Shia government, the Americans have been compelled to join sides with the Sunni insurgents who, as traditional rulers of Iraq, had been neither anti-American nor anti-West. They had only become so as a result of their disempowerment by the Americans when Saddam Hussein had been overthrown. The Sunni in their desperation to regain power had even joined with Al Qaeda extremists in an attempt to make Iraq ungovernable. The dramatic falls in the level of violence by the Sunni insurgents in the summer of 2007, and the unexpected decision by the Sunni tribal leaders to work with the Americans, gave a clear indication that the Americans had now sided with the Sunni and that they had abandoned their long-term goal of establishing democracy in Iraq. For their purpose in equipping and arming the Sunni tribes in Anbar province – including former Sunni insurgents, was not only to give the Sunni the ability to eliminate the Al Qaeda extremists in their midst, but also to give them the ability to regain political power in Iraq by military coup.

In adopting this fundamental change of policy, the Americans are following the example of the British. In the summer of 2007, the British Government, having declared that the Iraqis were now capable of good governance and could look after their own security, promptly withdrew their troops from Basra and concentrated their remaining forces into a single base at the airport from where it would be relatively easy to finally leave the country. This was done regardless of the true realities on the ground. The Americans have similarly recognised that after five years of devastation and violence, stability and order matter far more to the Iraqis than their form of political rule. Just as the British had accepted the desire of the American colonists in 1781 to run their own country in they way they choose, the Americans have now finally done the same thing for the Iraqi people. The neo-conservative American dream that peace and democracy can be spread around the world by force of military arms is at an end.

Following an American withdrawal, it is therefore likely that a Sunni/Kurd coalition will take power in Iraq. Neither group wishes to see an Iran-backed Shia government in control, nor indeed does America, and together a Sunni/Kurd alliance would prove militarily stronger than the Shia militias. This may not be the ideal solution from a Western liberal democratic perspective, and it would undoubtedly represent a second betrayal of the Shia. But whatever happens in Iraq, the final outcome will at least be an Iraqi solution, not one imposed by foreign powers.

As one of Rochambeau's aides said at the end of the American War of Independence, 'though the people of America might be conquered by well disciplined European troops, the country of America is unconquerable'. These words provide as fitting an epitaph for the folly that was Britain's war in North America in the eighteenth century as they do today for Bush and Blair's ill-judged war in Iraq.

Acknowledgements

During the lengthy gestation of *Washington's War*, I became indebted to many people who were kind enough to provide ideas and give advice. Above all, it was my long association with the National Securities Studies course at the Maxwell School of Citizenship and Public Affairs at Syracuse University, USA, that gave me the opportunity to develop my thoughts about the extraordinary parallel that exists between Great Britain's position as a global superpower in 1775 fighting an insurgency war in North America, and that of America today in Iraq. I am particularly indebted to Professor Stephen Webb of Syracuse University, whose great passion and intricate knowledge of America's eight-year battle for independence gave me the inspiration and enthusiasm to write this book. He was also good enough to read an early draft and suggest some important changes. I learnt much from the alumni of eight successive National Securities Studies courses, who, although I was often cast in the role of Johnny Burgoyne and even that of Michael Moore, treated me courteously but always challenged my views.

I am also grateful to John Dunbabin of my old Oxford College, St Edmund Hall, for suggesting an extensive reading list, and to Alice Rose for researching much of the important material that I have used. To give some balance to the book, I asked Professor Brian Holden Reid of King's

College London to read the final manuscript and he did so in the midst of a busy academic year. I am most grateful to him for his amendments. Mike Shaw, who had previously been my literary agent at Curtis Brown, also agreed to read the manuscript and he inevitably suggested many valuable changes. Without the persistence, patience and moral pressure from my superb editor at Weidenfeld & Nicolson, Keith Lowe, this book would never have been finished. I thank them all.

During the writing of this book, I maintained a long correspondence with one of the most outstanding American soldiers of his generation, a true Virginian, patriot and also long-standing friend, Colonel Bucky Burrus. If he had been one of George Washington's generals, I suspect that the British would have been forced to abandon the war in their American colonies a great deal sooner than they actually did.

Washington's War has ended up where neither I nor any of my mentors could have predicted. But as US Secretary of Defense Donald Rumsfeld once so famously observed, 'stuff happens'. I am therefore entirely responsible for the outcome of this book.

Finally, I am most of all indebted to Angela, my wife, who has had to put up with much during the past four years, but who has always encouraged and inspired me.

Bibliography

Alden, John R., *A History of the American Revolution* (New York, 1969)

Anderson, Fred, *Crucible of War* (New York, 2000)

Ayling, Stanley, *George the Third* (London, 1972)

Ballard, John R., *Fighting for Fallujah* (Connecticut, 2006)

Black, Jeremy, *War for America* (Stroud, 1991)

Black, Jeremy, *Britain as a Military Power* (London, 1999)

Bolton, Charles K., *The Private Soldier under Washington* (New York, 1997)

Brigham, Robert K., *Is Iraq Another Vietnam?* (New York, 2006)

Brumwell, Stephen, *Redcoats: The British Soldier and War in the Americas* (Cambridge, 2002)

Calhoon, Robert M., *The Loyalists in Revolutionary America* (New York, 1965)

Chandler, David, *The Art of Warfare in the Age of Marlborough* (Kent, 1976)

Conway, Stephen, *The British Isles and the War of American Independence* (Oxford, 2000)

Creasy, Edward, *The Fifteen Decisive Battles of the World* (London, 1903)

Dederer, John M., *Making Bricks without Straw* (Kansas, 1983)

Ellis, Joseph J., *His Excellency George Washington* (New York, 2004)

Enys, John, *The American Journals of Lieutenant John Enys* (Syracuse, 1976)

Fisher, H. A. L., *A History of Europe* (London, 1936)

Fortescue, Sir John, *The War of Independence* (London, 1911)

French, David, *The British Way in Warfare* (London, 1990)

Fuller, J. F. C., *The Conduct of War* (London, 1961)

Fuller, J. F. C., *Decisive Battles of the Western World* (London, 2003)

Gordon, Michael R., & Trainor, General Bernard E., *Cobra II* (New York, 2006)

Greene, Jerome A., *The Guns of Independence* (New York, 2005)

Guizot, M., *Monk and Washington* (London, 1851)

Hamilton, Edward P., *Fort Ticonderoga* (Massachusetts, 1964)

Harvey, Robert, *A Few Bloody Noses* (London, 2001)

Hashim, Ahmed S., *Insurgency and Counter-Insurgency in Iraq* (New York, 2006)

Headley, J. T., *Washington and His Generals* (New York, 1853)

Hibbert, Christopher, *Redcoats and Rebels* (London, 1990)

Higginbotham, Don, *George Washington and the American Military Tradition* (Georgia, 1985)

Houlding, J. A., *Fit for Service* (Oxford, 1981)

Irving, Washington, *George Washington* (New York, 1975)

Jenkins, Brian M., *Unconquerable Nation* (California, 2006)

Keegan, John, *A History of Warfare* (London, 1993)

Ketchum, Richard M., *Saratoga* (New York, 1997)

Lunt, James, *John Burgoyne of Saratoga* (London, 1976)

Macaulay, Lord, *Critical and Historical Essays* (London, 1872)

Macdonogh, Giles, *Frederick the Great* (London, 1999)

Mackesy, Piers, *The War for America* (Nebraska, 1964)

Mackinnon, David, *Origins and Services of the Coldstream Guards* (London, 1883)

McCullough, David, *John Adams* (New York, 2001)

McCullough, David, *1776* (New York, 2005)

Morrissey, Brendan, *Saratoga 1777* (Oxford, 2001)

Peabody, James B. (ed.), *John Adams: A Biography* (New York, 1973)

Peebles, John, *John Peebles' American War 1776–1782*, ed. Ira D. Gruber (London, 1997)

Rasmussen, William M. S., & Tilton, Robert S., *George Washington* (Virginia, 1999)

Reid, Stuart & Zlatich, Marko, *Soldiers of the Revolutionary War* (Oxford, 2002)

Reidesel, Baroness Friederike, *Letters and Journals* (New York, 2001)

Ricks, Thomas E., *Fiasco: The American Military Adventure in Iraq* (New York, 2006)

Rose, Alexander, *Washington's Spies* (New York, 2006)

Scheer, George F., & Rankin, Hugh F., *Rebels & Redcoats* (New York, 1957)

Shy, John, *Toward Lexington: The Role of the British Army in the Coming American Revolution* (Princeton, 1965)

Shy, John, *A People Armed and Numerous* (Oxford, 1976)

Tuchman, Barbara W., *The First Salute* (New York, 1998)

Willcox, William B., *Portrait of a General* (New York, 1964)

Wood, W. J., *Battles of the Revolutionary War* (North Carolina, 1995)

Wright, Esmond, *Washington and the American Revolution* (London, 1957)

Index

Abdul Qader, Gen, 153
Abercromby, Sir Ralph, 36–7
Abu Dhabi TV, 90
Abu Ghraib prison, 27, 117
Acland, Maj, 126, 128–9
Adams, John, 13, 46, 69, 77, 100
Adams, Samuel, 10, 46
Afghanistan, 21, 25, 33, 203
Al Jazeera TV, 90
al-Qaeda, 25, 207
al-Sadr, Moqtada, 150
al Zarqarwi, Abu Musab, 79, 151
Albany, 96, 125
Albemarle, Earl of, 48
Albright, Madeleine, 204
Allegheny Mountains, 11, 31, 38, 61
Allen, Ethan, 62
Amboy, 83
America, growth in, 31–2, 40
America's approach to insurgency in
   Iraq, 15–16
American Civil War, 202
American colonists, 10, 11–12, 13–15,
   16–17, 22
American Indians *see* Indians,
   American
American land reforms, 18, 31–2
American loyalists, 24–5, 47, 51, 61,
   65, 70–1, 107, 137, 171, 172
   oath of loyalty, 168–9
American state militias, 58–9, 90, 178,

179, 181, 182–3 *see also* individual
   entries
Amherst, Lord, 49, 104, 137
Anbar province, Iraq, 149, 151, 155, 156,
   207
Anburey, Lt , 124
André, Maj, 89, 173–4
Arbuthnot, Adm, 164, 165, 174, 175–6
Arnold, Gen Benedict, 62, 63, 65, 89,
   108, 112, 119, 122, 128, 130
   defection, 173–4, 175, 176, 178
Ashe, Gen John, 160
Assunpink Creek, 83
Augusta, 168, 180
Austrian forces, 35–6

Ba'ath Party, removing (de-
   Ba'athification), 17, 44, 60, 117,
   169
Baghdad, 42, 73, 75
Balkans, UN peacekeeping
   operations, 33
Barras, 191
Basra, 142, 150, 208
Baum, Lt Col Friedrich, 113, 114, 115
Beaufort, 162
Bemis Heights, 115, 119–20, 123, 124,
   127 *see also* Saratoga, battle of
Bennington, battle of (1777), 113,
   114–15, 132
Birmingham Meeting House, 102

213

Reed, Col Joseph, 81, 186–7
Reform Act (1832), 19, 201
'Regulator Rebellion', 146
Revolutionary War *see* War of
    Independence, American
Rhode Island, 88, 93, 140–2, 162,
    163–5, 173, 174, 175–6, 188
Richmond, 174
Riedesel, Maj Gen, 120, 123, 124, 126,
    129
Rochambeau, Count de, 164, 165, 188,
    189, 191
Rockingham, 196
Rodney, Adm, 173, 174, 189, 196
Rogers, Maj Robert, 38–9, 87, 113
Royal Navy, 36, 41, 47, 64, 66, 70, 71,
    99, 141, 142–3, 162, 164–5, 173, 174,
    188–9
  blockade, 133, 140
  Chesapeake Bay battle, 190–1
  press-gangs, 11
  sailors, 116
  after War of Independence, 201
  and Yorktown, 191, 192–3, 195
Rumsfeld, Donald, 20, 24, 44, 45, 56,
    59–60, 160

Sackett, Nathaniel, 88
Saddam Hussein, 17, 42, 44–5, 71, 73,
    78, 79, 104, 117, 148, 169
Sadr City, 150
St Augustine, 195
St Clair, Gen Arthur, 85, 110
St Leger, Lt Col Barry, 97, 110–11, 112
St Lucia, 139
Samarra, 151
Sanchez, Gen, 148, 150
Sandwich, Lord, 41
Saratoga, battle of (1777), 60, 83, 107,
    117, 152, 173, 181
  first battle (Freeman's Farm), 115,
    117, 119, 120–4
  second battle (Bemis Heights), 115,

119–20, 123, 124, 126–9, 130, 131,
    136–7
Sattler, Lt Gen, 155
Savannah, 144, 159, 195
  attack on (1779), 161–2
Savannah River, 159, 160
Saxe, Marshal de, 35
Schuyler, Maj Gen Philip, 62–3, 80,
    100, 110, 112
September 11, 2001, attacks, 25
Serbs, 35
Seven Years War, 29, 31, 35, 37, 38,
    49–50, 51, 68
Shelburne, Lord, 28
Shia Sadr militia, 150
Shia tribes, 14, 54, 71, 148, 150, 207,
    208
Skenesborough, 108, 109
Skippack Creek, 105
snipers, 128, 185–6
Spanish forces, 47, 196
Spanish Succession, War of , 35
Special Forces, Coalition, 39, 44
Stamp Act (1765), 48
Stark, John, 113–14, 115, 132
Staten Island, 70
Steuben, Baron von, 133
Stirling Lord, 81
strategy, failing, indicators of, 94–5
Stuart, Lt Col, 159
suicide bombers, 25, 53
Sullivan, Gen, 81–2, 102, 103, 141
Sullivan's Island, 71, 72
Sumter, Thomas, 169, 171
Sunni tribes, 14, 17, 54, 148, 150, 207,
    208
Syria, 134, 205

Taliban, 25
Tallmadge, Benjamin, 88
Tarleton, Lt Col Banastre, 168, 170,
    171, 176, 181, 182, 194
Tennessee frontiersmen, 172